The Missouri Supreme Court

Other Books by Gerald T. Dunne

Monetary Decisions of the Supreme Court
Justice Joseph Story and the Rise of the Supreme Court
Hugo Black and the Judicial Revolution
Grenville Clark: Public Citizen

The Missouri Supreme Court

FROM DRED SCOTT TO NANCY CRUZAN

Gerald T. Dunne

University of Missouri Press
Columbia and London

Library of Congress Cataloging-in-Publication Data

Dunne, Gerald T.
   The Missouri Supreme Court : from Dred Scott to Nancy Cruzan /
Gerald T. Dunne.
        p.   cm.
   Includes bibliographical references and index.
   ISBN 0-8262-0826-6
   1. Law—Missouri—History. 2. Missouri. Supreme Court—
History. 3. Missouri—Politics and government. I. Title.
KFM7878.D86   1992
347.778'035—dc20
[347.780735]   92-31525
                                                        CIP

Designer: Elizabeth K. Fett
Typesetter: Connell-Zeko Type & Graphics
Printer and Binder: Thomson-Shore, Inc.
Typeface: Trump Medieval

To my wife Nancy O'Neill Dunne, *1923–1988*

Contents

Preface

The best view of the Supreme Court of Missouri is from a plane. Seen from aloft, the court's Second Empire mansard-roofed and red-bricked structure (derided almost from the first as an "overgrown streetcar barn") contrasts starkly with the romanesque splendor of the nearby capitol and modern federalese housing the executive bureaucracy.[1] Interiorly, the contrast between new and old continues. A Victorian environment of polished mahogany, marble, and filigreed ironwork is encountered upon entry from a street-accessed ground story and ascends to the library on the second floor. The latter runs the entire length of the building with court rooms at either end. American primitive portraits of former members of the court, bearded and wire-spectacled, look down on visitors from the walls of the connecting corridor. At the east end a decorated courtroom provides the essential ceremonial centerpiece, and to the west, the second room offers a divisional, or secondary forum. Chambers—really apartments—are located on the second and third floors and recall an era when controversies took only part of the judges' time, thereby allowing them to continue their accustomed hometown residence while using

1. Bonnie Wright, Robert Durand Smith, and Haden D. Smith, "And So It Was Red: Missouri's New Supreme Court Building 1907," *Missouri Historical Review* 78 (1984): 414.

spartan bachelor quarters in the court building when actually hearing cases.

These apparent anachronisms persist into the late twentieth century. They are ironically appropriate, for the court is not only architecturally but functionally different from coordinate governmental branches. "The powers of the government shall be divided into three distinct departments, each of which shall be confided to a separate magistracy; and no person charged with the exercise of powers properly belonging to one of these departments, shall exercise any powers properly belonging to either of the others."[2] While constitutional democracy requires that the political branches of government be especially sensitive to the demands of each temporary majority, the third branch sits not to serve the wish of the present but to enforce the will of the past. There is a second force, parallel but not identical: the interplay between local self-government and the constraints laid upon it by the Constitution of the United States. From its earliest times, the Missouri Supreme Court has been caught in the tension between these two great forces. The resulting interaction forms a rich tapestry and, more than that, a perspective from which the lights and shadows of what has gone before can be glimpsed with a fresh acuity.

This attempt to create the view from that new perspective necessarily proceeds in a way that is episodic rather than lineal; it highlights, focuses on, and finds patterns and themes in the recurrent controversies that are resolved only to flow on into new conflicts after brief periods of repose. The overall pattern is essentially riparian, mirroring the flow of the two great rivers that has shaped the state's topography, its law and, indeed, its supreme court, which from circuit-riding beginnings has sat alongside them.

The biography of a legal institution inevitably presents a vision of law as a broad social and economic force. There is another dimension, however: the individual legacy of the one-hundred-and-seven incumbents who have sat on the bench of the highest court in their state, which suggests that the only certainty of law and history is that somehow men and women will make both.

2. "Of the Distribution of Powers," Mo. Const. art II (1820), in *Vernon's Annotated Missouri Statutes*, vol. 1 (St. Paul, MN: West Publishing Co.), 112.

Acknowledgments

It has been well said that an author who has gotten egg on his face will scarcely minimize it in a preliminary forewarning. Nonetheless, the convention is well established and should be observed, particularly in a book that is a plea for traditional values. Beyond apologies, it is also an opportunity for appreciation, and there is much to be expressed. Priority goes to The Supreme Court of Missouri Historical Society, which commissioned the work, and to its special Literary Committee, which diligently examined preliminary drafts under the chairmanship of Stuart (Tim) Symington, Jr. Errors of fact, grammar, or nuance that have survived such diligent oversight remain the responsibility of the author.

Especial thanks are due to the author's onetime student, Mr. Joseph Fred Benson, for a close and critical reading of the text, and to his research assistants, Gao Tong and Andrea Lamere. However, the greatest debt of gratitude is owed the St. Louis University Law School, to former Dean Rudolph Hasl, and to Ms. Shirley A. Moore of the faculty secretaries. Both the latter helped make the writing of this book a labor of love and thereby heightened the author's affection for his native state and appreciation of the privilege of being the chronicler of its high court.

BEGINNINGS

1

Headwaters

THE RIVERS

The wedding of two great rivers shaped Missouri, its institutions, and its law. The first river, aptly the Father of Waters, split the continent; the second, the Great Muddy, rose in the continental divide, cut southeasterly and then met its spouse in the state that bore the Indian name for its massive, silt-filled presence, Missouri. As observers from Father Marquette to Jonathan Raban have noted, the meeting is not a blending but a collision. The clash of the waters is marked by spume, whirlpool, and immense forces of destruction; after the conflict eventually spends itself, the merged rivers briefly settle into a seeming harmony. The cycle of collision and concord is a striking symbol for the law of the state as developed by its supreme tribunal and political assembly—the character of which itself grew out of other meetings that occurred within the boundaries of the state: races, classes, cultures, and legal systems. Like the rivers that were their prototypes, these forces began as a conflict that was eventually resolved into a confluence only to emerge in conflict once again.

THE INDIANS

Missouri also provided the meeting place for two great Indian cultures. The Siouan in the continental west was exemplified by the Osage and Missouri bands in the center of the state. The con-

1

tinentally eastern Algonquian was represented by the Kaskas who had migrated to the juncture of the Meramec and Mississippi rivers. Speaking languages as distinct as Swedish and Italian, and representing the varied cultures of the plains dwellers and the forest peoples, neither cultural group was savage, although tragically for them their technology of violence was primitive alongside that of the displacing Europeans. Indeed, both Indian groups had complex and sophisticated legal systems that provided rules for personal property, marriage, and dispute settlement. Common to both systems was a blind spot on land ownership, a concept that stood at the center of all European jurisprudence, and provided, in the European view, the very foundation for property, politics, and political power. As Tecumseh interprets the Indian ethos: "Sell a country! Why not sell the air, the clouds and the great sea, as well as the earth? Did not the Great Spirit make them all for the use of his children?"[1]

This conflict in perception was the virtual extinction of the Indian law on Missouri soil. The great American commentator James Kent summarizes the process:

> The European nations which respectively established colonies in America, assumed the ultimate dominion to be in themselves, and claimed the exclusive right to grant a title to the soil, subject only to the Indian right of occupancy. The natives were admitted to be the rightful occupants of the soil, with a legal as well as just claim to retain possession of it, and to use it according to their own discretion, though not to dispose of the soil at their own will, except to the government claiming the right of pre-emption. . . . The United States adopted the same principle, and their exclusive right to extinguish the Indian title by purchase or conquest, and to grant the soil, and exercise such a degree of sovereignty as circumstances required, has never been judicially questioned.[2]

The ambiguous phrase, "extinguishing the Indian title," a staple

1. Section 14 in John Bartlett, *Familiar Quotations*, 15th ed. (Boston: Little, Brown, 1980), 419.
2. James Kent, *Commentaries on American Law*, 379. Indeed, only in the jurisprudence of marriage did Indian law leave a trace in Missouri as its supreme court, following Justice Joseph Story and Henry Schoolcraft, validated tribal marriages, even polygamous and possibly incestuous ones, between Americans and Indians. Johnson v. Johnson, 30 Mo. 72 (1860); Buchanan v. Harvey, 35 Mo. 276 (1864).

of both federal and Missouri law, implies that the Indians did indeed have rights, which were at best those of mere occupancy subject to an almost inexorable suppression. This guaranteed that, aside from a few place names and probate matters, no trace of Indian law would survive in the context of the displacing European culture.

ROMAN LAW
The French and the Spanish

Only historians know that the streets of early St. Louis were once ruled by the *Coutume de Paris*;[3] it was a legal system drawn from the same Roman codes that formed the basis of the Spanish legal system, and was brought to the trans-Mississippi West when the Louisiana Territory was transferred from France to Spain in 1762. The transfer was more nominal than real. The territory continued to be culturally French, and the few professional lawyers in what became Missouri were trained by the French, coming upriver from New Orleans. Their practice continued even under Spanish rule, with the first Spanish governor being careful to make no changes in the existing system. Such enlightened imperialism could last just so long. The second governor, Don Alejandro O'Reilly, a quintessential Spanish conquistador despite his Irish name, came under orders to integrate the territory that is now Louisiana and Missouri into Spanish America. In 1769, he decreed that the Louisiana territory be ruled under the same laws as the rest of the Spanish empire, that judicial proceedings be in Spanish, and (in unconscious testimony to the common Roman law heritage of the two cultures) that proceedings be heard by an appointed tribunal composed of judges trained in both French and Spanish law. It was a vain gesture. The sheer pressure of events decreed that everyday life go on as before and when the law did intrude upon personal affairs, it came in the form of the imperfect French legacy which outlasted the essentially transitory Spanish jurisdiction.

3. The *Coutume*, a grouping of 362 titles written in 1510 ("Nos Edits, Ordonnances Et Coutoumes Et les Usages de la Prevosté Et Vicomté de Paris"), theoretically applied to all colonial possessions of France. See Morris Arnold, *Unequal Laws unto a Savage Race*, 11.

AMERICANIZATION

Producing a displacement similar to the dissolution of the aboriginal Indian law, the great migration of 1810–1820 brought droves of Americans, white and black, into upper Louisiana through the Ohio River from the upper tier of the American South. The migration completely changed the host area and the law along with it. Notably, the immigrants included American lawyers who chose to establish themselves in a new land, a new sovereignty, and a new legal system.

Sheer weight of numbers supplanted the French culture and its legal overlay. Just as English crowded out French as the language of the streets, English legal ideas displaced the French in everyday transactions such as marriage, juries, mortgages, and inheritance. Even before the actual Louisiana Purchase, Jefferson foresaw that the transaction would, as to the acquired territory, "turn all their laws topsy-turvy."[4] A number of American lawyers came to upper Louisiana even before the Louisiana Purchase. A larger number came after it, even though they were migrating to what might be, with respect to the law, permanently alien territory. Article XXXII of the Purchase treaty confirmed the inhabitants of the Louisiana Territory to the rights of person, property, and religion. Clearly Article XXXII applied to real property rights (a matter of much future litigation), and arguably at least to all rights cognizable under the civil law.

Nonetheless, the influx of lawyers trained in the common law of England and the political institutions involved in the cession produced a pressure for change too great to be resisted. By the end of 1815, the question of "what laws shall be in force in this territory," as a local paper called the issue, had reached priority status. It was far more than a question of "what laws." Rather it was a way of looking at the law that had split Europe—and European foundation in the New World—like a fault line. On one side lay the ancient Roman codes, an all-encompassing coverage whose despotism was mitigated by a laxity of enforcement and a practice of frequent dispensation. On the other side rested English

4. Letter, dated November 9, 1803, from President Thomas Jefferson to James Gallatin, quoted in George Dargo's *Jefferson's Louisiana*, 107.

common law, a collection of judge-made rules sifted down to razor-sharp fineness in successive controversies that resulted in a dynamic process rather than a comprehensive command. "When new problems arise," the court of King's Bench summed up the genius of the common law in 1769, "new principles will be discovered to resolve them."[5]

The "reception" of the common law in Missouri really began with incremental procedural changes passed by the territorial legislature—mortgages, conveyances, and wills—which placed a common law stamp on accustomed ways of doing things.[6] The statute of wills destroyed the Latin idea of forced heirship, replacing it with the English concept of the unfettered disposition of property and the unlimited right of a father to disinherit children. Moreover, both mortgages and wills moved from ponderous ceremonial formality to simple signatory execution. Especially significant were the Anglo-Saxon transplantations engrafted onto the Latin system: habeas corpus, trial by jury, and prohibition of cruel and unusual punishments.

The formal changeover started with a motion by Congressman Caulk in the Territorial Legislature on January 5, 1816. The house gave the report of the committee of the whole a favorable 16–8 vote (interestingly, the one identifiable Frenchman voted against the proposal with American newcomers on both sides of the question). The legislative council (a de facto upper house) concurred, and the common law crossed the Mississippi on January 19, 1816, in a statute still in force but whose meaning was litigated in the late twentieth century:

> The common law of England, which is of a general nature, and all statutes made by the British parliament in aid of or to supply the defects of the said common law, made prior to the fourth year of James the first, and of a general nature, and not local to that kingdom, which said common law and statutes are not contrary to the laws of this territory, and not repugnant to, nor inconsistent with the constitution

5. *Missouri Gazette*, February 3, 1816; Millar v. Taylor, 98 Eng. Rep. 201 (K.B. 1769).

6. See Conveyances 1 Mo. Territorial Laws 46 (1804) (Law to establish Recorder's Office); 1 Mo. Territorial Laws 125 (1807) (Wills, Descent, and Distribution).

and laws of the United States shall be the rule of decision in this territory.[7]

Of all the conflicts inherent in the legacy of Missouri law—civil law and common law, local right v. central constitution—the most marked dissonance came in the internal dynamics of the common law itself: the desirability of stability, continuity, and certainty *versus* the organic need for adoption to new circumstances. The contradiction was summed up in two maxims carved in the stone of the supreme court's building. One proclaims, "Jus dicere non dare"—that the judge should *pronounce* but not *give* the law; the other states, "Ubi jus, ibi remedium"—where there is a right, there is a remedy. The contradictory command to seek continuously to do justice in new ways but within a context of stability and continuity echoes through the colliding impact of the two great rivers and appropriately summarizes the past—and the future—of the state's law and its medium, the high court.

7. 1 Mo. Territorial Laws 436 (1816). See also Jones v. State Highway Comm'n, 557 S.W.2d 225 (Mo. en banc 1977).

2

Flawed Foundations

CORNERSTONES

A congressional enabling act signed by president Madison in 1818 authorized the territory of Missouri to organize a state government as a preliminary to admission to the Union. Accordingly, delegates to a constitutional convention met in the dining room of Mansion House, a St. Louis hotel, on June 30, 1820. Their task was to lay the legal foundations of a new state; in the process they also almost guaranteed that Missouri would not become one.

THE COURTS

In structuring the judiciary, the convention followed the grand design of the United States Constitution and provided for an appointive judiciary selected by the governor—a three-member supreme court, circuit courts, and such inferior tribunals as the General Assembly might later set up. Judicial service was for life—almost. Sitting judges held their place during good behavior and were protected against salary diminution while they held office. Even though the draftsmen borrowed heavily from Kentucky, two provisions were apparently taken from the New York Constitution of 1777: the office of the chancellor and compulsory retirement of judges at age sixty. The ongoing application of the English common law was ensured by an obscure addendum (called a "schedule") that enforced the enactments of the territorial legislature, thereby extending the "reception" statute of 1816.[1]

The provision for a chancellor was to prove a bad mistake. The office had been given lustre by its great New York incumbents; one, Robert Livingston, was eulogized privately by no less than President Franklin D. Roosevelt: "Robert Livingston was the chancellor of New York who swore in George Washington [as president]. He was a great jurist and a great student of the law. He contributed much to juridical literature and legal knowledge."[2] Alas, lustre could not be transplanted. The office of chancellor never really took hold here for a variety of reasons and did not last out the first decade of Missouri's statehood.

THE CURSE OF COLOR

Another decision of the constitutional convention was to have more profound legal consequences. It concerned the issue of caste and color, which was to prove an abiding curse for the new state. Blacks had lived in Missouri before the first permanent white settlement. Their arrival meant no improvement in their condition because they were being brought as slaves from the West Indies by the French to work the lead mines. They left little trace of either themselves or their labors. More permanent was the legacy of the free men of color, largely of Santo Domingo origin, who were included in Laclede's expedition to found St. Louis.[3] French indifference to color doubtless accounted for the failure to list their race on the expedition manifests, but Anglo-Saxon neurosis on the point underscored the legal ambiguity of the free black community when the American flag went up over St. Louis on April 4, 1804. Capt. Amos Stoddard, who raised the flag, had words

1. Mo. Const. art. V (1820). See the discussion of the New York 1777 constitution in Francis Thorpe, ed., *The Federal and State Constitutions*, 2635. Mo. Const. (1820) "Schedule."

2. Claude Pepper, *Pepper: Eyewitness to a Century*, 62. The president added that Livingston was an ancestor of Mrs. Roosevelt.

3. We have no record of the number of free black "hired men" who accompanied Laclede to St. Louis and who stayed over. However, the fairly widespread practice of freeing slaves by will toward the end of the eighteenth century did provide the nucleus of a free black community in town. Interview by author with Rev. Barnabas Faherty, S.J., January 2, 1988.

of assurance for the French inhabitants and the Indians present, but none whatever for the cluster of blacks in the crowd.

That perception, manifesting a conviction of inferiority and unassimilability, was written into the proposed Missouri constitution by the drafting committee. The passage came before the convention on June 30, 1820: "The general assembly shall have no power to pass laws, . . . For the emancipation of slaves. . . . It shall be their duty, as soon as may be, to pass such laws as may be necessary . . . To prevent free negroes and mulattoes from coming to, and settling in this state, under any pretext whatsoever."[4] The clause occasioned little stir but the institution of slavery did. John B. C. Lucas published a rare French handbill ("Aux Electeurs Du Compte De St. Louis")[5] suggesting the impossible: retention of patriarchal household bondage, but prohibition of its large-scale plantation form. At the convention an amendatory suggestion to require the removal of emancipated slaves from the state failed by a vote of 27 to 13. Characteristic of the ambiguity enshrouding the entire subject was another provision, which passed with only one negative vote, enjoining that criminal punishment of slaves be equivalent to that inflicted on white persons for similar crimes.

This exclusion clause came near to aborting Missouri's admission to the Union. The minutes of the state constitutional convention show no consideration whatsoever was given to the compatibility of the clause with Section 2 of Article IV of the U.S. Constitution, which says the citizens of each state should possess the privileges and immunities of citizens in the several states, such as protection from the disabilities of alienage. At this time citizenship, a term of undefined content, was largely a state matter, and if a state bestowed citizenship on blacks, there was little under the U.S. Constitution that Missouri could do to bar them from free passage to, or residence on, Missouri soil. Senator Burrill of Rhode Island urged yet another constitutional objection

4. Mo. Const. art. III, 26 (1820); see also *Journal of the Missouri State Convention* (1820) 18, Joint Collection, University of Missouri and Western Historical Manuscript Collection, State Historical Society of Missouri, Columbia, Missouri.

5. April 20, 1820, Archives, State Historical Society of Missouri, Columbia, Missouri.

clause—contravention of the national war power: "It was well-known that we have colored soldiers and sailors and good ones too, but under no pretext whether of duty or motive can they enter Missouri."[6]

The delegates should have been forewarned. The mere suggestion that slavery, thought by many to be a dying institution, should get a new lease on life had already touched off a fire storm in Congress; one commentator found it significant that the original constitution never so much as mentioned slaves and slavery by name: "Somehow, the fathers and fashioners of this basic document of liberty hoped that the reprobated institution would in time pass away when there should be no verbal survival as a memorial of its previous existence."[7] Hence, Missouri's statehood formally established slavery west of the Mississippi and even confirmed it there, which triggered protests in and out of Congress. Up in Salem, Massachusetts, Justice Joseph Story made the only political speech of his court career to protest the extension of slavery; the aging Jefferson declared that controversy filled him with the apprehension of hearing a fire bell in the night ringing the death knell of the Union.

The first effort to secure admission of the state with the tainted constitution failed. A distinguished historian has pointed out the anomaly where the first so-called Missouri Compromise (whereby Maine was admitted as free state and Missouri as a slave jurisdiction) has historically overshadowed the far more substantive second one neutralizing the exclusion clause.[8] All the skills of Henry Clay were required to salvage Missouri's admission. By it, a congressional reservation provided admission only if Missouri would by "solemn public act" promise that the exclusion clause would never be applied to abrogate constitutional rights.[9] President Monroe was empowered to determine compliance. The first session of the new state legislature sulkily complied, and on July 17, 1821, James Monroe, in possible violation of the explicit letter of the Constitution, declared Missouri a member of the Union, and

6. *Annals of Congress*, vol. 37, 16th Cong., 2d sess., December 4, 1821, 47.
7. Kelly Miller quoted in Gunnar Myrdal, *An American Dilemma*, 86.
8. Don E. Fehrenbacher, *The Dred Scott Case*, 102.
9. S. Con. Res. 1, 16th Cong., 2d sess. (1821).

it thus became the only state ever admitted by plenary presidential proclamation.[10]

Missouri's two senators and one representative, having cooled their heels in anterooms while the offending constitution was debated, were admitted to the legislative chambers and picked up their pay for the entire session.

JUDICIAL GENESIS

A less controversial portion of Missouri's 1820 constitution was Article VI "Of the Judicial Power." Pursuant to his appointment power, Governor Alexander McNair moved with reasonable promptitude to construct the first supreme court with three appointments. Senior appointee and "president" (as entitled by the rules of court) and de facto chief justice—even though the title would not emerge constitutionally for some time—was Matthias McGirk. A thirty-one-year-old Tennessean who was serving as senator from St. Louis County, McGirk was a solid choice. Trained in the common law of England, he was a sponsor of the 1816 territorial statute whereby that common law was received as the law of Missouri. He had been a member of the territorial council (really the upper house of the territorial legislature) and served on the court until 1841 where his disproportionate number of opinions became a powerfully stabilizing force in the institutional structure of the new tribunal.

The second appointee was Virginian John D. Cook of Ste. Genevieve. He, too, had been trained in the common law prior to his arrival in Missouri; he had come west with George Rogers Clark's rangers in the capture of Vincennes. His service was short (and undistinguished), as he resigned in 1823, but subsequently served as a circuit judge, United States attorney, and private practitioner.

Judge Cook had another distinction—he was probably the ugliest man to ever sit on the Missouri Supreme Court:

> Judge Cook was an extremely ugly-looking man, and, what is strange, seemed to regard his repulsive looks as a fortunate gift. Upon one occasion he was selected . . . to represent Cape Girardeau in [a]

10. 1821, Mo. Laws Ch. 311, 2; James D. Richardson, ed., *Messages and Papers of the President,* 664.

Convention which was held in Chicago . . . [he] took passage on a steamer for St. Louis, and one of the party discovered a gentleman on board uglier than Judge Cook. This gentleman proved to be Judge Wight, a distinguished man from Ohio, and on his way to the same convention. On returning to his party [the discoverer] offered to bet a bottle of wine that there was a man on board who was uglier than Judge Cook. A stranger overhearing the conversation, and who was an acquaintance of Wight, immediately turned his eye upon Cook, and said, "I will take that bet," and it was agreed that it should be decided by a disinterested committee of three: it was then proposed to bring about an introduction between the two judges, and when it took place each fixed his eye most intently upon the other for several seconds without a word passing between them. At length Judge Cook broke silence by saying, "Judge Wight, before I left home I promised that if during my absence I found a man uglier than myself, I would immediately return; and now, sir, I shall leave the boat at the next landing." "Stop, my dear sir," said Judge Wight "you may be a good judge of law, but you are an exceedingly poor judge of beauty. . . . I propose to let the bar decide it;" thereupon they all proceeded to the *bar*, and over several bottles of champagne drank to each other's health; and it was *held*, without a *dissenting opinion* . . . that two uglier men were never born of woman, and they should be adjudged to pay the *costs.*[11]

The third appointee was Pike County's John Rice Jones, a Welshman and Oxford graduate from Washington County. A trenchant writer, he was the court's first outstanding dissenter with his peppery idiosyncratic disagreements leavening the otherwise dull content of the early state reports. His junior status meant he was last in order on the routing list and constrained his writing time, which he plainly disliked: "The argument of this case not having been through until late on Tuesday evening and the Court being about to adjourn this day, has put it out of my power to give an opinion at large on the case."[12] Even though the junior appointee, he was senior in years and escaped compulsory retirement by dying in office on February 1, 1824.

Particularly interesting was the Missouri chancellorship, an office with traditional equity powers and statewide jurisdiction. It did not readily transplant and died on Missouri soil. The ter-

11. William V. Bay, *Reminiscences of the Bench and Bar of Missouri*, 47.
12. Price v. Rector, 1 Mo. 74, 78 (1821); Holmes & Eliot v. Carr & Co., 1 Mo. 41, 43 (1821).

ritorial jurisdiction was too vast and unwieldy, and the rising democratic impulse across the young republic was inhospitable to juryless equity. Moreover, the office easily became involved in whether it should mitigate the common law harshness of mortgage delinquencies. Missouri's first (and only) chancellor, William Harper, doubtless did his best in the few years following his appointment; however, that effort was foredoomed. Both houses of the state legislature vied with each other to dismantle the office, which was abolished by constitutional amendment in 1825. Harper returned to his native South Carolina where he became an ardent exponent of nullification and used his Missouri titles, probably to good effect, in proclaiming and writing forceful screeds to present the separatist doctrine.[13]

THE COURT'S FIRST HOME

Also following English precedent was the character of the state's high court as an itinerant tribunal. The initial statute required that it sit for successive terms in the river towns of St. Charles, St. Louis, Franklin (since destroyed by the river), and Jackson. Given the scant resources and primitive state of a frontier society, scattered and permanent quarters were an impossibility, and the court sat where and as its needs could be accommodated by the county circuit court. Time has destroyed the early records, but surviving evidence suggests that the first sitting probably came at a ramshackle courthouse in St. Louis on April 29, 1821. Notably, the judicial inauguration went unnoticed in the *Missouri Gazette, St. Louis Enquirer, The Missourian* (St. Charles), and the *Gazette* (St. Joseph).

The court got off to a bad start. The first entry in its general minute book in the case of *Hanly v. Holmes* recorded that "the transcript in this case is either lost or mislaid that it cannot now be found. It is ruled by the court that the Clerk of the Circuit Court of the County of St. Louis certify to this Court in a complete transcript of the record of proceedings had in the said cause."[14]

13. See "Judge Harper's Speech Before the Charleston State Rights Association" (1831) and "The Remedy of State Interposition or Nullification" (1832), South Carolina Historical Society, Charleston, South Carolina.
14. April 3, 1821, General Minute Book of the Supreme Court of Missouri, Missouri Historical Society, St. Louis, Missouri.

The first supreme court house. Courtesy of State Historical Society of Missouri, Columbia.

The loss of the record was quickly repaired, but the sequences of constitutional crises that lay ahead would not be as easily composed, given the tension between the first state constitution and the organic law of the United States. There lay a context of conflict for the new state, its law, and its high court for the first years of existence of all three.

GROWING PAINS

3

Funny Money

Experience taught Missouri little. Indeed, the same insensitivity to the commands of the U.S. Constitution, which had almost aborted her admission to the Union, seemed to persist unabated as the territory assumed the powers of a state. Three trips to the United States Supreme Court were required to adjust the parochial impulses of the new polity to the requirements of the national constitution. Moreover, the three trips provided special insight on the interplay between the supreme courts of the state and the nation.

The first trip resulted from the crunching economic turndown which beset the entire country almost simultaneously with Missouri's admission to the Union in 1820–1821. Distress came with the backwash of the panic of 1819 and embodied the classic signs of hard times. Ready cash disappeared as hoarding became the household response to economic stringency. Land values plummeted, and economic duress made once indulgent creditors turn to seizure and dispossession to collect their debts. Immigration stopped as well as land clearance and home building. The legislative reaction was classic too; it sought, among other things, to put more money in circulation and tempered foreclosure by setting floors below which property could not be sold for debt.[1] The

1. See W. J. Hamilton, "The Relief Movement in Missouri 1820–1822," and James Neal Primm, *Economic Policy in the Development of a Western State, Missouri, 1820–1860.*

latter remedy was short-term relief, being a purely ameliorative check on the wave of foreclosure. The first, however, looked to general relief as a sort of precursor of the later Greenback and Populist remedies. Both responses were embodied in laws passed at a special "relief" session of the General Assembly unenthusiastically called by the governor in the summer of 1821 and in the regular session that followed. Clearly, something had to be done. As "Old Farmer" wrote in the *Missouri Gazette* the preceding April 21, "Never was there in this country a time of so much pecuniary distress as the present."[2] The stay law provided that appraisers would be appointed prior to any foreclosure to evaluate the endangered property. Unless the creditor agreed to take the property at two-thirds of such appraised value in full payment of his debt, foreclosure could not be undertaken for two and a half years.[3] The companion statute was a truly imaginative idea that provided for paper money and that contemplated replacing Missouri's only bank, now insolvent, with state "loan offices," which would issue "loan certificates" backed by the credit of the state and secured by its salt springs.[4] The state had to take such certificates for taxes and, ultimately, so did foreclosing mortgagees,[5] who were required to accept them in payment of their loans.

On the face of it, the "stay" law was a patent violation of the U.S. Constitution to which Missouri became subject upon its admission to the Union. The law was obviously inconsistent with Article I, Section 10, which forbade any state from passing an ex post facto law, from impairing the obligation of contract, or from making anything but gold and silver legal tender in payment of debt. The "loan office" act seemed equally infirm by providing a state with paper money. Nonetheless, the remedy was welcome, "the public will, no doubt, learn with pleasure" announced the *St. Louis Inquirer* on September 1, 1821, "the paper of this institution will soon be thrown into circulation. . . . The eagerly wished for *relief* will make its appearance."

2. Primm, *Economic Policy*, 2 n. 1.
3. 1821 Mo. Laws Ch. 349.
4. The frontier value placed on salt as a preservative in a marginal society is carried in many Missouri artifacts; for example, the very name of Saline County.
5. 1821 Mo. Laws Ch. 313

FIRST PASS AT ARMS

The stay law was quickly challenged, and the new state supreme court showed its temper writing seriatim opinions as the judges seemed to outdo each other in probing the federal flaws of the legislation. The action came when a mortgagee challenged the part of the valuation provision by reducing his debt for three-fourths its value.[6]

The Missouri Supreme Court exemplified the newly hatched doctrine of judicial review (whereby the court purported to void a statute in toto rather than merely refusing to enforce it). John Dillard Cook was uneasily defensive, insisting that the court did not usurp legislative power in violation of the state constitution by voiding the statute for repugnance of that of the United States. Appealing to *Marbury v. Madison*, he noted that Article VI of the U.S. Constitution required every state judge to swear allegiance thereto and to enforce it. It followed that the law was void, not because the court so pronounced it, but because the legislature was prohibited from passing any such enactment in the first place. Chief Justice McGirk joined in the annulment, explicitly resting his condemnation on Article VI (federal supremacy) of the U.S. Constitution as a national instrument.

CONSTITUTIONAL CONFRONTATION

While the stay law was reprobated at the state level, the loan office certificates excited concerns nationally. No effort was made to bring the decision on the stay law before the U.S. Supreme Court (in view of the limited grounds then prevailing), and consequently the adverse ruling of the state tribunal became final.

The loan office act was a horse of another color. Local circuit courts were substantially united in condemnation of it notwithstanding newspaper approval.[7] There was local applause: "Our judiciary" offered a toast at a conservative dinner: "May they never shrink from the duty imposed on them by the establishment of a

---

6. Baily v. Gentry, 1 Mo. 116 (1822).

7. One circuit condemnation was delivered by Nathan Beverly Tucker, celebrated jurist and future William and Mary professor in Missouri v. William Carr Lane in the St. Louis Circuit Court.

loan office by declaring it unconstitutional."[8] Its basic constitutional infirmity was seen in the splintered decision at the state
level. At issue was the character and status of the interest-bearing
"loan certificates" authorized by the statute. Were they "bills of
credit" prohibited by Article I, Section 10, of the United States
Constitution? Missouri's monetary needs were obvious. Indeed,
the necessity of gold and silver substitutes were foreseen in Article VIII of the state's first constitution, which explicitly provided
for a note-issuing bank. Equally obvious were the ideas of the
founding fathers who were unmistakably determined to put the
states out of the paper money business once and for all. Their
mindset was clearly indicated from Edmund Randolph's keynote
address at the constitutional convention to Madison's excoria-
tion of "bills of credit" in the Forty-fourth Federalist Paper (1788).[9]
Such a context clarified the framers' intent despite obscure language. Their constitutional prohibition had worked so well that
by the early nineteenth century, state paper money had virtually
disappeared from the American scene and the framers' term "bill
of credit" had likewise vanished from the American political
vocabulary.

Nevertheless, this semantic ambiguity was resurrected when
three borrowers who had gotten $199 from a loan office refused to
repay on the ground that the consideration was illegal, namely,
because the Constitution prohibited bills of credit. The Circuit
Court of Chariton County disagreed and ordered repayment in
the state's collection suit. The thorny question came in for decision in the state supreme court's 1824 term at Jackson. The court
divided as it found more than enough constitutional infirmities
to go round. McGirk declared that the paper, in substance, was
illegal bills of credit and correspondingly found the supporting
contract utterly void. Judge George Tompkins went the other way
and found the loan certificates and the mortgage contract valid.
Judge Rufus Pettibone decided in favor of constitutionality holding that the character of the legal tender (whereby a creditor was
forced to take the certificates in satisfaction of debt or lose post-

8. Quoted in Wilbert Rosin, "Hamilton Rowan Gamble" (Ph.D. diss., University of Missouri, 1960), 47.
9. Gerald T. Dunne, *Monetary Decisions of the Supreme Court* (New
Brunswick: Rutgers University Press, 1960), 11–12.

tender interest) was necessary to outlaw the loan office certificates. There was only a partial legal tender here. For, as noted above, only foreclosing mortgagees, the tax-collecting state, and unpaid public employees *had* to take the certificates or, in effect, impair their claim. Otherwise creditors were free to accept or reject them.[10] Indeed many merchants had already advertised that they would not do so.

Under the slow state of transportation and communication, it took five years for the case to get to Washington. The Supreme Court called it up on writ of error with the argument being held at the 1830 term. Senator Thomas Hart Benton appeared in defense of the statute, regardless of his abhorrence of paper money, summed up in his nickname, "Old Bullion." As a Jacksonian, Benton was almost as hostile to the judicial imperialism, and his plea was essentially a technical one that the case was not properly before the Supreme Court by not complying with the limited grounds for appeal.

Typically, Chief Justice Marshall ignored the marginal issues and went for the jugular in language whose force concealed the wafer-thin (4–3) division of his tribunal. After reviewing the havoc produced by pre-constitutional inflation, he pronounced the loan office statute null and void and reversed the judgment of the Missouri Supreme Court: "To cut up this mischief by the roots . . . the people declared in their Constitution that no State should emit bills of credit. If the prohibition means anything, if the words are not empty sounds, it must comprehend the emission of any paper medium by a State government for the purpose of common circulation."[11] It was the first reversal of Missouri public policy by the nation's high tribunal and, as such, a portent of things to come.

10. Mansker, Graves and Simpson v. State, 1 Mo. 321 (1824); State v. Craig, 1 Mo. 356 (1825).
11. Craig v. Missouri, 29 U.S. (4 Pet.) 410, 432 (1830).

4

Missouri Soil

Five years after the public policy of Missouri was first weighed and found wanting by the U.S. Supreme Court,[1] Missouri law was again examined by the nation's high tribunal in the case of *Chouteau's Heirs v. United States.*[2] This conflict was far more difficult and subtle than the fairly obvious collision of the Missouri relief legislation and the commands of the United States Constitution. At issue were the values and insights of the two great legal systems of Europe. These were the common law of England and the civil law of Rome as exported to the prairies of the North American continent.

The focus of the conflict was land. The distinctive perceptions have been well summarized by a comparative law analyst:

> In English law, historically, and still theoretically, only the Crown can own land. The intricate system of freehold estates fashioned by common law technicians is based not on ownership of land but on an abstraction called an estate, a time in the land. . . .
>
> In contrast to the common law, the civil law system of property is based on the idea of absolute undivided ownership. No "estate" is interposed between the owner and his property.[3]

1. See *supra*, n. 11 at 21.
2. 34 U.S. (9 Pet.) 137 (1835).
3. Henry P. de Vries, *Civil Law and the Anglo American Lawyer: A Case-Illustration & Introduction to Civil Law Institutions and Method* (Dobbs Ferry: Oceana, 1976), 365.

The royal Spanish Louisiana domain in America was not to be sold but rather to be given away for surveying costs to suitable settlers of demonstrated character and stability, for example, Catholic artisans and farmers whose presence would form a bulwark against English expansion in the trans-Mississippi West. Indeed, it would have been culturally inconceivable for either His Catholic or Most Christian Majesty (to give the Spanish and French monarchs their formal titles) to become real estate hucksters trafficking in a land office business. The procedure of largesse was theoretically simple but productive of immense subsequent difficulties.

The apex of the Spanish system, which prevailed between 1762 and 1803, was a captain general in far-away Havana. He was assisted by a governor general in New Orleans, who had jurisdiction in civil and military matters, and by an intendant who administered revenue and admiralty. Further complexity was introduced by repeated combination and redivision of the offices, successive promulgation and repeal of land grant regulations, and conflicting pronouncements as to delegated authority.

The baroque legal overlay contemplated a complex land grant procedure in upper Louisiana, an area that ultimately would become territory and state. The first step was approval by the on-the-spot military commander of a present or prospective settler's application for occupancy of a designated tract of land. The commander would then forward the favorably endorsed application to the lieutenant governor in St. Louis. At that point the latter functionary would issue a "cession" (describing the land involved) and an order of survey to the royal surveyor general. The survey document and plot would be then entered in the surveyor's register, a virtually secret registry. The last step—and the cause of much future trouble—was that the cession be formalized by approval of the governor general in New Orleans, thereby making it a royal grant. In practice, the primitive state and inordinate delays of river communications resulted in the virtual disregard of New Orleans approval. As such, unperfected cessions were routinely bought, sold, occupied, and inherited in upper Louisiana with only a handful of land titles being formally perfected.

Unlike the noblesse oblige of the French and Spanish monarchs, the land law of the young American republic was rapaciously opportunistic. Here, public lands were seen as a national treasure to be openly sold by land offices as expeditiously as possible. A federal surveyor general mapped the whole nation into townships and sections, and the soil was offered for cash. The conflict that arose from these policies and latent claims of earlier occupants—the Indian occupancy was disregarded—has been well described by Professor Lawrence Friedman: "No chain of title could escape federal land policy, any more than the lots and farms could ignore the merciless, invisible grids stretched over the land at government order."[4]

An exemption to the grids was set out in the agreement whereby Louisiana was transferred to the United States and whereby also the inhabitants of the ceded territory were "protected in the free enjoyment of their liberty, property, and religion."[5] Presumably, the reference to "property" included the quasi-secret and unperfected Spanish grants frequently obtained by fraud, rarely occupied, and subject to unfulfilled conditions. Shortly after the Louisiana purchase, Congress enacted the first of an extended and flip-flopping sequence[6] of laws undertaking to balance the claims of bona fide settlers, who had followed local custom in ignoring the technicalities of Spanish law, and still deal appropriately with flagrant frauds. A special board of commissioners was instituted to pass on Spanish land claims. Appeals from adverse decisions of the commission were permitted to the federal district court in St. Louis.

The separately established federal ladder implicated a severance of national and local perceptions. In the nature of the case, the ordinary business of life entailed wills, sales, and leases in which Spanish grants became part of the law of the case.[7] Generally, the local courts (including the lower-level federal tribunal) tended to treat the unperfected "cession" transfer as void.

4. Lawrence Friedman, *A History of American Law* (New York: Simon & Schuster, 1973), 203.

5. Art. III, Louisiana Purchase Treaty, Francis Thorpe, ed., *The Federal and State Constitutions* 3:66.

6. See Act of March 26, 1804, Ch. 38, 2 Stat. 283, 287–89; Act of March 3, 1807, Ch. 36, 2 Stat. 440; Act of March 12, 1814, Ch. 52, 3 Stat. 121; Act of May 26, 1824, Ch. 173, 4 Stat. 52; Act of May 24, 1828, Ch. 90, 4 Stat. 298.

7. See Clark v. Brazeau, 1 Mo. 208 (1823); Vasseur v. Benton, 1 Mo. 212 (1823); George v. Murphy, 1 Mo. 558 (1827); Hill v. Wright, 3 Mo. 175 (1833).

On frequent occasions, Spanish grants were litigated before the U.S. Supreme Court. Here, section 3 of the Franco-American transfer treaty safeguarding the habitants in their property provided a difficulty. Luke Lawless, storm center of the St. Louis bar and paladin of flawed Spanish titles, argued that the imperfect grants ("which the Supreme Court of Missouri speaks with such contempt," Lawless once noted)[8] were property beyond the power of the United States to annul, either directly or by requiring validation by a board of land commissioners. The issue was finally settled at the national level by de facto validation of the Spanish claims.

A typical confrontation was *Chouteau's Heirs v. United States*,[9] a case which began in 1800 when Auguste Chouteau petitioned the Spanish lieutenant governor for title to a designated tract of land, which was duly granted and confirmed by the governor general. Chouteau in due course requested the American board of commissioners to validate his title; his request was denied, and the issue of the validity of title was taken to the United States District Court of Missouri. An adverse verdict for Chouteau there ultimately came before the Supreme Court.

In interesting contrast, Marshall's reaction to the land controversy was very different from his almost apodictic response to Missouri's paper money, doubtless due to experience with the post-Revolution inflation. In an obviously irascible disposition of the pipsqueak frontier controversy that had intruded on the serious business of his court, Marshall summarily ended the matter. Under his analysis, the ultimate question in the case became the Spanish lieutenant governor's authority to give Chouteau title. Without undertaking a detailed analysis of Spanish law, the chief justice examined the documentary evidence and (in an essentially common law twist) used custom and usage to decide the civil law controversy—that the lieutenant governor in St. Louis was indeed the authorized agent of the governor general in New Orleans— and that in consequence, Chouteau's title "according to . . . the general understanding and usage of Louisiana and Missouri . . . is . . . to be held as sacred and inviolate as other property."[10]

8. Barry v. Gamble, 44 U.S. (3 How.) 32, 37 (1845).
9. 34 U.S. (9 Pet.) 137 (1835).
10. *Id.* at 145.

An interesting by-product of the arcane Spanish land grant procedure appeared in the impeachment of James Peck, federal district judge in Missouri. In the extended series of statutes to regularize Spanish land grants, Congress gave his court jurisdiction to resolve Spanish claims. One such was that of Antoine Soulard for a vast amount of territory ceded by Spanish Lieutenant Governor Zenon Trudeau in 1796. (Trudeau, it might be noted, was alleged to have signed a number of blank sheets of paper, which were presumably to be filled in post hoc as "cessions.") Moreover, applicable Spanish law contemplated that such cessions would be made only for services to His Catholic Majesty.

A question as to "the authority of (Trudeau) to make cessions" caused Peck to reject Soulard's claim. Luke Lawless, wrote to the *Missouri-Advocate* criticizing the decision. (Lawless was a major litigator for Spanish claimants.) Peck took exception to Lawless's tone, ordered him to prison for twenty-four hours and disbarred him from the federal district court for eighteen months. Lawless was released on a state writ of habeas corpus from jail, and Peck was impeached by the House of Representatives for oppression in office; he was acquitted when the vote (21–22) in the Senate found him not guilty. Peck was probably unbalanced: He frequently appeared in court blindfolded (because of an aberrational fear of sunlight), judged witness credibility by smell, and required documentary evidence to be read to him by the clerk or counsel. For his handling of Lawless, he was impeached by the House of Representatives, tried by the Senate, and escaped ouster when the latter body failed to convict; the minority vote fell short of the constitutionally required supermajority.[11]

---

11. See generally Arthur Litz, "Spanish Land Grants and New Madrid Certificates," 23 J. Mo. B. 206 (1967); Walter B. Stevens, *Centennial History of Missouri*, 1, 14; Keltner Locke, "A Peck of Trouble," 50–60; and Arthur J. Stansbury, *Report of the Trial of James H. Peck* (Boston: Hilliard, Gray & Co., 1833).

5

The Red and the Black

The compiler of statutes had no intention of using layout to underscore Missouri's besetting moral problem, but he did so nonetheless when he chose to caption a section of the *Revised and Digested Statutes of the State of Missouri* (1825) with a clarion call that was the centerpiece of the American creed:

Freedom
An act to enable persons held in slavery to sue for their freedom.

The statute was a remarkable five-part law passed on December 30, 1824, by the General Assembly. Legislative journals are silent on the sponsorship and lack any comment on the proposal. Even more remarkable in view of the law's blockbuster content and moral judgment is the contemporary silence of newspapers who were wont to speak out vigorously on every item of public interest. In spite of being such a fireball, it was routinely passed, duly signed, published, and promulgated.

Throughout the United States an undercurrent of resistance to the dominant slave culture was manifesting itself in "freedom" statutes, permitting wrongfully enslaved persons to sue for emancipation. But Missouri's law was something special, in terms of both content and procedure.[1] Basically, the act provided that any person wrongfully detained as a slave could petition the local cir-

1. See Don E. Fehrenbacher, *The Dred Scott Case*, 61.

cuit court, stating the ground of grievance, and empowering the court—should the petition in the opinion of the court contain "sufficient matter" (the undefined content of the phrase was to be a matter of mischief)—to order that a full-dress trial with counsel assigned to the slave plaintiff at public expense. In addition, the court might prohibit removal of the alleged slave from its jurisdiction and punish reprisal by the putative master during litigation.

The latter section was further expanded by providing the plaintiff reasonable liberty in attending court and conferring with counsel and binding the owner to ensure such access. Another section required due regard for "written evidence" but also recognized that "such other proofs" might be required in these cases and provided for a "judgment of liberation." Interestingly, the law was made effective July 4, 1825.

In March of 1825, Isaac McGirk, prominent member of the St. Louis bar and brother of the state's chief justice, anticipated the effective date of the statute by filing a freedom suit thereunder on behalf of Catiche, a slave held by Jean Pierre Chouteau, Sr.[2] The suit was but one part of a sequence of litigation that already stretched back twenty years and would go forward almost twenty more by being tried in the St. Louis, St. Charles, and Jefferson County circuit courts, with several hearings in the Missouri Supreme Court, until finally going to the United States Supreme Court itself. The litigation also symbolized both the Indian tragedy and the special degradation inflicted on women by the slave system.

The pivotal question concerned the color of the plaintiff. Was Catiche red or black? The answer was indeterminate; she was both, being one-quarter of one race and three-quarters of the other. Actually the slave code defined her as "mulatto," a person with one African grandparent, even though "all other progenitors shall have been white."[3] Beyond that the questions grew more complex since enslavement of blacks was authorized by both French and Spanish law, but Indians were guaranteed freedom under the latter.

2. Catiche, a Person of Colour v. Chouteau, Minute Book 4:349–50, Circuit Court of St. Louis.
3. 1818 Mo. Territorial Law 28 (1809).

An especially difficult legal issue was presented by the cession of Louisiana from France to Spain in 1762 and the promulgation of Spanish law in the territory by Spanish Governor O'Reilly in 1769. Did enslaved Indians become free automatically?[4] And when Louisiana went back to France was the sequence reversed? Even more difficult was whether article 3 of the treaty, which transferred Louisiana to the United States and safeguarded the inhabitants in their "liberty, property, and religion," covered an Indian slave's right to freedom *or* the owner's right to service? Little wonder that the courts returned inconsistent answers to the issues when presented with a mare's nest of legal and ethical choices. The territorial executives, both Spanish and American, also waffled, and it took a characteristically hammer-stroke opinion of Chief Justice John Marshall to put the whole matter to rest.

Who was Catiche? Allegedly, she was the granddaughter of a Natchez Indian, Marie Jean, who had been brought to Fort Chartres near St. Louis after French policy had decreed the extermination of the rebellious Natchez nation. Most of the surviving Natchez were shipped as slaves to Santo Domingo, but Marie was taken north to Chartres. There a union with a Negro slave, Sypion, produced a daughter, Marie Jean; the latter wound up in St. Louis as something of pawn in the proprietary and familial complexities of the patriarchal Chouteau family, whose interest extended not only to Marie Jean, but her three daughters (also by Negro slaves) Catiche, Celeste, and Marguerite. Even though nominally owned (if she were owned at all) by a Chouteau in-law, the suit of Catiche was directed at the head of the clan—Jean Pierre Chouteau, Sr., himself.

Whether McGirk had a stake in the suit based on a more intimate entanglement in the immorality of slavery is suggested by the subsequent bequest of his residuary estate to his chief justice brother in trust for Brunetta, "the daughter of a free woman of color, Harriet."[5] Not surprisingly, Circuit Judge Alexander Stuart

4. *Caeteris paribus*, the answer seems "no." See L. S. Rowe, *The Political and Legal Aspects of a Change of Sovereignty*, 41 American Law Register 466 (1902).

5. See Charles Van Ravensway, "Matthias McGirk," 8 *Bulletin of the Missouri Historical Society* (1952): 224 n. 3. The will itself is in the archives of the Missouri Historical Society, St. Louis, Missouri.

dismissed the petition, holding that the standard of "sufficient matter" had not been met. Undeterred, Isaac McGirk went to the Missouri Supreme Court, not by appeal (a point of concern only to lawyers) but to seek an original writ of mandamus commanding the trial court to do what the law seemed plainly to order and implicitly to hold—that mere allegations without proof conferred jurisdiction. Apparently, his brother, the chief justice, did not sit on the mandamus case. The writ was granted.

The case went back to the St. Louis circuit court for a hearing held by a new judge who appointed McGirk, Hamilton Gamble (future governor and supreme court judge) as well as circuit attorney Faris as lawyers for Catiche. The trial court's subconscious sympathy was evident by the formidable battery of lawyers appointed. But another roadblock emerged in a judgment handed down some twenty years earlier by the territorial court that had found Catiche to be a slave. This would have foreclosed any future litigation of that issue as res judicata, but Catiche and her lawyers sought yet another writ of mandamus on the ground that the circuit court should grant a full-dress trial and not settle matters on a preliminary point.

They got their second writ from Judge Tompkins (again Chief Justice McGirk apparently did not sit), who ordered the case tried and decided on the basis of the circuit court's *own* records ("But we are willing to admit, that the Circuit Court has a right to resort to the records of another court")[6] and not those elsewhere. The statute accorded enormous judicial discretion, and Tompkins's antislavery instinct (which earned him the sarcastic encomium "apostle of freedom" in the subsequent *Dred Scott* litigation)[7] performed predictably. Tompkins seemed on solid ground in reversing the territorial tribunal, which had, in fact, blown hot and cold on the issue of the plaintiff's status by both authorizing her freedom and acquiescing in her limited detention.

Tompkins's reversal of the trial court initiated a second round of litigation which began in 1826 in the Circuit Court of St. Louis. Several suits were now involved: Catiche's original action proceeded, and Catiche's sister Marguerite took center stage and sued

6. Catiche v. Circuit Court, 1 Mo. 434, 435 (1826).
7. Fehrenbacher, *Dred Scott*, 61 n. 1.

Chouteau for *her* freedom.[8] McGirk and Gamble represented all plaintiffs under court appointment; a formidable defense team, Luke Lawless and Henry Geyer, argued for Chouteau. The evidence on all sides was shaky as to Marguerite's Indian grandmother: "Some of the witnesses stated that they had heard aged persons say that she was of the Natchez nation."[9] The legal issues were complex, but the pivot of the case was the effect of the transfer of Louisiana from France to Spain in 1762 and the necessarily retroactive effect of the Spanish law of Indian freedom. Beneath the verbiage was the significant issue suggested by the high-powered legal teams that had been assembled: the possession of one drop of Indian blood, even if established by the most suspect of double hearsay, might suffice to get a plaintiff to a sympathetic jury and possible emancipation.

Alas, for Marguerite the instructions of the court to the jury went quite the other way, virtually predetermining the verdict by providing that the slave status of an Indian claimant that survived transfer of Louisiana to Spain continued under Spanish rule and continued under the American flag. Accordingly, the jury found for Chouteau.

On appeal, the Missouri Supreme Court (McGirk still apparently not sitting) divided evenly; in the light of the one-to-one deadlock, the verdict stood. However, in 1833 by agreement of the parties the appeal was heard again before a full court, and this time McGirk did participate and silently sided with Judge Tompkins's erudite and lengthy opinion, which reversed the circuit court's judgment for error in the jury instruction and ordered a new trial.[10] Judge Robert Wash dissented in a much shorter statement asserting that notwithstanding territorial transfer, the rights of the owners of Indian slaves "are secured and protected as well by the law of nations as by the express stipulations of the cession to the United States."[11] While technically right, he was substantively wrong.[12] The shuttlecock case was initially set for a new trial in St. Charles County but ultimately transferred to Jefferson

8. Minute Book 4:249–50, Circuit Court of St. Louis.
9. Marguerite v. Chouteau, 3 Mo. 375, 375 (1834).
10. *Id.* at 392.
11. *Id.* at 395.
12. See L. S. Rowe, "The Political and Legal Aspects," 466 n. 4.

County. There, after two trials, the jury followed the revised instructions and set Marguerite free. The result was routinely affirmed by the Missouri Supreme Court.

The stakes on the emancipation potential of the Tompkins's
view were high enough to warrant appeal to the Unites States
Supreme Court, and review was duly sought. Chouteau retained
Thomas Hart Benton and Francis Scott Key to appeal. Marguerite's counsel sought to avoid a Supreme Court judgment on the
principal "drop of Indian blood" issue. B. F. Butler, a Washington
lawyer and part-time U.S. attorney general who had taken Marguerite's side on the appeal for $250, wrote St. Louis counsel
Hamilton Gamble as to the judiciousness of raising the question
of jurisdiction: "I think the court will be glad to avoid the main
argument."[13]

He was right. Chief Justice John Marshall dismissed the appeal for want of jurisdiction, a highly technical point.[14] The chief
justice also indicated his displeasure with taking his court's time
for a parochial matter that had been twice litigated to jury verdict. The anonymous dismissal held that the Franco-American
treaty of cession was not involved in the suit. That could be said,
but in another view, its nuanced overtones were the very heart of
the case. The true heart, however, was the fact that in January
1838 almost a third of a century after the issue was first litigated
before the Missouri territorial court, Marguerite received in Washington, D.C., that which the state statute promised: Freedom.

13. B. F. Butler to Hamilton Gamble, March 6, 1838, Gamble Papers, Missouri Historical Society, St. Louis.
14. Choteau [sic] v. Marguerite, 37 U.S. (12 Pet.) 507 (1838).

MIDCENTURY
TRANSITION

6

Admiralty

BEGINNINGS

The mere presence of the Mississippi and Missouri rivers as the principal arterial throughways of the Louisiana Territory precipitated early legal problems. Probably the first admiralty case in the area was *Pouree v. Chouteau*. In early 1782 Pouree, a bateau carrier, received freight from Chouteau for carriage from New Orleans to St. Louis, "subject to the ordinary conditions of carriage by water." Depredations of the English pirates and Indians along the river route required delay, detours, and safe-passage payments. Pouree sued Chouteau for these extra costs in the lieutenant governor's court in St. Louis; the latter functionary, following customary practice, called in three arbitrators. These seem to have split the difference, awarding Pouree some but not all of the asserted extra charges.[1]

THE GREAT TAKEOVER

Pouree provided an apt opening to the years preceding the great upheaval of the Civil War. These might well be likened to an unforeseen Mississippi whirlpool: formless, turbulent, and embody-

---

1. Arnold Morris, *Unequal Laws unto a Savage Race*, 63–64. Notably, this seems also the first recorded arbitration, anticipating by two centuries the Missouri Uniform Arbitration Act; Mo. Rev. Stat. 435.350 to .470 (1985).

ing forces that seemed to work at cross-purposes to each other. The process of change in these forces was fuelled by technology. Here, the instrument was the steamboat, which afforded a tremendous breakthrough in compacting the vastness of both the young republic and the still younger state. Communication and transport were vastly improved both in cost and quality, but there were drawbacks. The boiler-propelled wooden steamboats were subject to frequent explosion, which threw fire and splinters with projectile-like force against crew, passengers, and cargo. Moreover, the complex machinery required frequent repairs, and being a mobile and valuable item of property, it might be hundreds of miles away by the time an unpaid artisan or merchant was even aware of the disappearance.

Historically, the law of the sea admiralty had addressed itself to these problems. The law had been born in ancient Rhodes, matured in the maritime states of Venice and Genoa, and was brought to England by Eleanor of Aquitaine when she came to marry Henry II. It was shaped by its environment; in it the ship was personified as a entity, and damages were limited to the vessel's value. Compared to the ponderous slowness of the common law, admiralty's juryless procedure was simple, streamlined, and summary on the theory that ships were meant to sail, not stay tied up at the dock during long litigation.

Moreover, when transplanted to England, admiralty came into conflict with the common law. The absence of clear demarcation between fresh and salt water was matched in a wavering boundary between the courts of admiralty and of the countryside. The latter held a general jurisdiction over transactions within the kingdom and especially over the land disputes, which were its matrix. But how about transactions that were concluded on land and performed at sea? These included insurance policies and bills of lading, all the very stuff of the rising sea-borne commerce quite apart from seaman's wages, ship repairs, and harbor collisions that had been admiralty's daily bread. In England there were preliminary passes at arms between the admiral (who was both a civil and military officer) and the judges of the common law. The tension produced poisonous hostility; the situations in which two jurisdictions coexisted in the same territory could only be compared to two chefs trying to cook in one kitchen. In England the controversy was resolved by the flat application of political power: in 1389 Parliament decreed that the admiral "shall not meddle henceforth of anything done within the realm but only of things done on the sea."[2] The statute was not literally applied— admiralty continued its role over seamen's wages and maritime repairs, contracts obviously made ashore, but like anything else, the tide's high-water mark (London Bridge in England) marked the territorial end of its rule.

This was manifestly the original understanding when the founding fathers wrote the Constitution in 1787, assigning "admiralty and maritime jurisdiction" to the newly organized federal courts and away from state tribunals. Congress, however, did not go quite that far; local tension marked the grant of federal jurisdiction under the first judiciary act in the qualification, "saving to suitors" any remedy at common law when the common law was competent to give it.[3]

The balance was upset by the powerful centralizing impulse of commerce and technology, which produced a sequence of judicial and congressional amendments of the United States Constitution. The first step came in 1815 when the circuit court decision of Justice Joseph Story repealed the old English statute (as far as the U.S. was concerned) and held that federal admiralty jurisdiction extended to land-prepared maritime documents such as insurance policies and bills of lading. When the opportunity came, he refused to follow up this *functional* extension with a *geographical* one, holding (in a federal suit for riverman's wages for a voyage up the Missouri) that federal jurisdiction was limited by the "tidewater" boundary of the original understanding. However, in 1845 Congress (in a statute drafted by Justice Story, who had previously blown hot and cold on the constitutional limitation) extended federal jurisdiction from the saltwater of its traditional domain to the freshwater of the navigable inland rivers and lakes. While some grumbling came from inland states who suddenly found themselves maritime ones, the federal coup generally had grass-roots support.

Remarkably, the Missouri legislature, disposed to protest every

2. 13 Richard II, St. 1, c. 5 (1389).
3. Act of Sep. 24, 1787, Ch. 20, 9, 1 Stat. 73, 77.

invasion of the state's rights and memorialized Congress accordingly, was silent. The aggrandizement of jurisdiction was upheld by the Supreme Court, Chief Justice Taney asserting that American need—not traditional English precedent—was in the minds of the constitutional draftsmen when they formed the organic law of the republic. More than that, the Supreme Court held, in an exuberantly nationalist opinion in *The Hine*, a case involving a steamboat collision near St. Louis, that the 1845 statute made federal jurisdiction exclusive. Notably, however, the federal coup of 1845 again saved "a concurrent remedy at the common law where it is competent to give it *and* any concurrent remedy" given by state laws where such steamer or other vessel was employed in essentially local commerce and navigation.[4]

The proviso recognized the obvious inapplicability of European solutions. Aware that the elaborate European registry system was irrelevant to a one in which a craftsman could assemble a raft or bateau in a few hours, Judge Robert Wash of the Missouri Supreme Court foresaw that "the law applicable to ships and sea-going vessels, is no way applicable to flat boats and fresh-water craft."[5] In its 1837 Boats and Vessels Act, Missouri granted a lien to creditors of local steamboat enterprises; however, in an interesting sequence of decisions, the Missouri Supreme Court confined the law to voyages on Missouri waters and refused to endorse its extraterritorial application. While Missouri seemingly acquiesced in 1845 to the federal amputation of its legitimate constitutional powers, its supreme court in a subtle pre–Civil War riposte exhibited a nuanced distinction between land agreements and maritime contracts.[6]

The Hine opinion (obviously a product of Union triumphalism) triggered a series of debtor defenses to lien collections under the Missouri statute. Here the state supreme court rolled with

4. Act of Feb. 26, 1845, Ch. 20, 5 Stat. 726, 727; The Steamboat Thomas Jefferson, 23 U.S. (10 Wheat.) 428 (1825); The Propeller Genesee Chief, 53 U.S. (12 How.) 443 (1851); The Hine v. Trevor, 71 (4 Wall.) U.S. 555 (1866); DeLovio v. Boit, 7 Fed. Cas. 418 (D. Mass. 1815) (No. 3,776).

5. Johnson v. Strader, 3 Mo. 254, 256 (1834).

6. James v. The Steamboat Pawnee, 19 Mo. 517 (1854); Twitchel v. The Steamboat Missouri, 12 Mo. 412 (1849); The Steamboat Raritan v. Pollard, 10 Mo. 583 (1847).

the punches in conceding federal supremacy and exclusivity but insisted the controverted lien "was a land contract, [even] though relating to a vessel, and not a maritime [one]."[7] Justice Samuel Miller of the U.S. Supreme Court was spared from reversing himself on the exaggerated overtones of *Hine* when he silently agreed by side stepping the appeal on a technicality and permitted the Missouri assertion of local autonomy to stand on a de facto affirmance.[8]

---

7. Boylan v. The Steamboat Victory, 40 Mo. 244, 252 (1867).
8. The Victory, 73 U.S. (6 Wall.) 382, 383 (1867).

7

Field Comes to Missouri

Submit Dickinson Field may well have been the most important woman in the law of the nineteenth century. She bore nine children. Of her six boys, one became the intellectual and moral leader of the midcentury United States Supreme Court, another built the Atlantic cable, and a third reformed American law, massively and significantly.

Lawyers frequently divide law between substance and procedure. Substance is the legal rules themselves; procedure is the method by which the legal rules are given effect. There are those who say that the latter is the more important—that a right without an effective remedy is no right at all—and up to the mid-nineteenth century effective remedies could be a very difficult business. Enforcement of the right—whether reparation for a broken promise or damages for a physical injury—followed different routes in the courts of law as to assertion, defense, and resolution. More problematic than this was the enormous gulf that separated law and equity—two bodies of rules with separate procedures, remedies, and sometimes, as Missouri started out, with separate courts.

In 1848 Submit's son David Dudley Field persuaded the state of New York to adopt a comprehensive and systematic "code" that radically simplified and streamlined court procedures. The "Field Code" did away with special remedies in the law courts and filled in the chasm separating law and equity by abolishing special courts of equity and requiring all claims, legal and equitable, to be tried in the law courts. According to Field, all legal controversies divided themselves into three stages: allegation, proof, and decision. The allegations, he noted, were made by pleadings. Under the old English common law, a litigant was required at his peril to pick out the correct label (called a "form of action") for the assertion of right contained in his petition to the court. If the court determined that the latter had picked the wrong form of action, the litigant ran the risk of having his case thrown out of court. Pleadings were originally short and simple, but over the centuries they have undergone a profound mutation, becoming "long, over-loaded with verbiage, uncouth phrases and endless repetition."[1] The process of pleading became so complex that it created a new kind of lawyer, the "special pleader," who made his living drafting pleadings that would stand up in court.

Even worse, Field said, was the common law requirement that proof conform strictly to the pleadings, a requirement that similarly led to "repetitions, pleonasms and to the introduction of different counts as different ways of stating the same case."[2] Field proposed a simple and effective remedy: that a litigant be required to state his complaint, briefly, in plain language and without repetition. Field enacted this great reform into law by embodying in his code a collection of the rules for entering and proceeding in court.

After passage in New York, Field's code took root next in Missouri (1849) and California (1851). Professor Lawrence Friedman suggests why: "Both states had some remnants of civil law in their background. Both entered the Union with a history of land controversies and a full docket of land-grant problems. These land claims could not be analyzed as legal or equitable; the distinction was meaningless and procedurally disruptive."[3]

The man who brought the Field Code to Missouri was Judge

1. David Field, "What Shall Be Done with Practice in the Courts?" in Stephen Presser and Jamail Zainaldin, *Law and American History* (St. Paul: West & Co., 1980), 408.

2. *Id.*

3. Lawrence Friedman, *History of American Law* (New York: Simon & Schuster, 1973), 343–44.

Robert William Wells, a Virginian who succeeded the stormy James Peck on the federal district court after a record tenure as Missouri attorney general (1826–1836). Like Field, Wells had long chaffed under the inadequacies of the existing legal system. By 1847 he had published his plan for abbreviating assertion of legal rights, for shortening the record made in cases, and for combining law and equity. Moreover, he supported his idea with a powerful plea in the court of public opinion through a pamphlet, "Law Reform," which was warmly applauded by the *United States Magazine and Democratic Review* both as to its substance and authorship. The latter publication hailed the assault on the "hoary fabric of pedantry and obscurity, the source of extensive litigation, uncertain law and public injury." In 1849 when the Field Code was introduced into the General Assembly, Wells appeared before the state senate and debated the code's merit. Wells's great work was encompassed in a statute containing thirty-two "articles" whose preamble declared its three goals: "Whereas it is expedient that the present forms of actions and pleadings in cases at common law should be abolished; that the distinction between legal and equitable remedies should no longer exist; and that an uniform course of proceedings in all cases should be established."[4]

The heart of the matter was set out in Article VI requiring "a statement of the facts . . . in ordinary and concise language, without repetition, and in such manner as to enable a person of common understanding to know what is intended."[5] The legislature passed the proposal, and on February 24, 1849, Governor Austin King approved the bill.[6]

Law reform—the first of many efforts—had at last come to Missouri. It was all part of a larger effort within the common law world (wherein the self-reforming nature of that jurisprudence also appeared in the English Civil Procedure Act of 1833) whereby justice, formerly expensive and delayed was made cheap and available.

4. 1849 Mo. Laws 73.

5. *Id.* at 79.

6. Roy T. King, "Robert Wells, Jurist, Public Servant, and Designer of the State Seal."

8

Judging the Judges

The framers of the first Missouri Constitution followed the example of their contemporaries elsewhere in organizing the judicial arm of their new state. Elective judiciaries in 1820 were a rarity. About half the state legislatures held the power of judicial appointment. In the remainder, executive appointment (with legislative approval) was the rule. It was the latter provision that was written into the U.S. Constitution. Another inherited tradition—this one from the English Act of Settlement of 1701—dictated that American judges hold their office *quam diu bene gesserant* (while behaving themselves well); it was occasionally linked with age compulsory retirement. The result of these influences were reflected in Article V of the Missouri Constitution of 1820: "The governor shall nominate, and by and with the advice and consent of the senate, appoint the judges of the supreme court, the judges of the circuit courts, and the chancellor, each of whom shall hold his office during good behavior."[1]

An attempt to subject judicial power to the democratic process appeared in a proposal at the constitutional convention to limit judges to a six-year term. The proposal was easily defeated, but efforts continued in the first session of the Missouri legislature to move the appointing power from the governor to the General Assembly with selection by joint vote at fixed intervals. This pro-

1. Mo. Const. art. V, 13 (1820).

posal was also defeated. The judicial veto of the 1820–1821 relief program also fueled efforts to curb a politically irresponsible judiciary (see chap. 3). These efforts continued into the succeeding second General Assembly where Edward Bates, future attorney general for Abraham Lincoln, eloquently stated the opposition case to "unsettl[ing] the balance of the government by making the judicial department dependent in all things on the legislature." Another political candidate stated the rebuttal, assailing the newly hatched power of judicial review as "[un]warrantable and dictatorial power in declaring laws . . . unconstitutional."[2]

Unquestionably, the abolition of the Missouri chancellorship was an incidental by-product of the effort to make the judges heel. This action was followed by a decade of calm; indeed, it was not until a legislative session in 1832 that the democratic tide flowed in the proposal to amend the Missouri Constitution and select the judges of the state supreme court for a six-year term by a joint vote of the legislature. Circuit judges were to be chosen for a lifetime by the voters of their circuits. Even though passed by a majority in the General Assembly, the proposals failed to obtain the constitutionally required two-thirds legislative vote and were never submitted to the people.

Restiveness appeared in an 1834 amendment to the state constitution that ended life tenure and provided for gubernatorial appointment to a three-year term. Thereafter the rising democratic tide, as exemplified by the politics of Andrew Jackson, began to flow with a vengeance and picked up an irresistible momentum in efforts to convene a state constitutional convention with the prime purpose of ending judicial life tenure by way of periodic electoral choice. The result was the constitutional convention of 1845 that proposed fixing the supreme court at three members to be appointed by the governor to twelve-year terms.

The proposed constitution was defeated at the polls in August 1846, but the effort to integrate the business of judging and politics continued. The democratic movement continued extending the electoral process to the offices of secretary of state, attorney general, state auditor (all previously gubernatorial appointees and de facto members of a "cabinet") and limiting judges to a twelve-

2. Jack Pettison, "Missouri Plan for the Selection of Judges," 15, 16.

year elected term. The problem was not resolved, however, only deferred. Finally in 1850 democracy triumphed. The judges of the state supreme court became elective officers with six-year terms.[3] Missouri's great historian, Floyd Shoemaker, summarizes the effort with characteristic style and lucidity: "Of the three departments of [state] government the judiciary of the state was the last to succumb to the levelling spirit of democracy."[4]

The issue of whether too great a price was paid for the triumph of the democratic doctrine appeared in the summer of 1851, when the elections for the state supreme court became something of a referendum on the politics of Senator Thomas Hart Benton. As a result, two of the three judges were defeated and the new court, chosen in a flawed process, was called to deal with *Dred Scott*, the most momentous issue in its institutional history.

3. To this day Missouri elects subordinate executives, such as secretary of state, attorney general, treasurer, and even state auditor.
4. Floyd C. Shoemaker, *Missouri's Struggle for Statehood, 1804–1821*, 123.

9

Judges, Senators, and Cur Dogs

The 1850 landmark change in judicial selection (whereby periodic voter choice replaced lifetime tenure) necessarily enmeshed the Missouri Supreme Court in politics. The change only recognized the obvious for the court was already badly enmeshed. One element was Judge James Birch's stump speech that defamed Thomas Hart Benton, United States senator and uncrowned king of Missouri; Benton responded by accusing the jurist of meretricious conduct with a slave girl. The Birch-Benton controversy began in 1849, a full year before the scheduled senatorial election as Benton began to sink in the quicksand of the slavery controversy. After Birch had spoken against Benton's reelection the senator responded: "I wonder when the damned scoundrel whipped his wife last?" That was the least offensive of Benton's rejoinders; more opprobrious was the vituperation of both Birch and his associates: "The Platte City clique have brought Jim Birch—that cur dog—yes, that son of a cur—yes, a damned sheep-killing dog— to speak against me; since I was at Liberty he has whipped his wife . . . all for keeping his own negro wench."[1]

By these words, Benton charged Birch with the crimes of mayhem and adultery. Birch promptly sued in the Circuit Court of Henry County. Unquestionably, the charged political content of the controversy and the uncertain character of the unfolding law

1. Birch v. Benton, 26 Mo. 153, 155–56 (1858).

46

of defamation accounted for the snail's pace of the proceedings. The trial was not concluded until 1853 when Birch got a $5,000 verdict. The appeal dragged on until 1858 (after both parties were dead) when the Missouri Supreme Court (per Judge Richardson, Scott concurring, and Napton not sitting) reversed Birch's judgment by reason of a variance between pleading and proof in a tedious second technical opinion that was a light year away from the Field Code.[2]

Worse yet in terms of judicial politics was the action of Napton in drawing the "Jackson Resolutions" (which took its name from proslavery extremist, Claibourne Jackson)—an extreme proslavery view of the then current constitutional controversy, ostensibly cast in the form of instruction to Missouri's senators:

> That the territories acquired by the blood and treasure of the whole nation ought to be governed for the common benefit of the people of all the States. . . .
> . . . that in the event of the passage of any act of congress conflicting with the principles herein expressed, Missouri will be found in hearty co-operation with the slave holding States in such measures as may be deemed necessary for our mutual protection against the encroachments of northern fanacism.[3]

Napton actually boasted that he wrote every line of the resolutions and did so in his chambers. Moreover, he later asked that the authorship be inscribed on his tombstone, oblivious to the fact that the subject of his screed could (and indeed would) come before him for judgment. Also typical of the politicizing of the court at the end of 1850s was Judge John F. Ryland's disclosure to his mentor, Senator Benton, of the views and prospective votes of his two colleagues on the bench.

The slavery issue necessarily colored the senatorial election of 1850. Benton, who had represented Missouri from its admission (and, technically, even before that) for an unprecedented thirty years, was involved in the fight of his life. A swarm of judicial aspirants ran either for or against Napton as senatorial election necessarily flowed over into the judicial one. Curiously, there were accusations that many entered the political arena merely to

2. *Id.* Perhaps Napton's recusal resulted from his avowed hostility to Benton.
3. Joint Resolution, 15th Leg., 1848 Mo. Laws 667.

demonstrate the evils of an elective judiciary by demonstrating their own unfitness.[4]

In a confused result, the old lion Benton went down to defeat. A splintered legislature finally chose Henry Geyer as his successor, the decision not coming until early 1851. Even though the constitutional provision providing popular selection of judges deliberately placed that process a year after the general political election, the insulation proved ineffective in mid-nineteenth-century Missouri. The fallout from the Benton election persisted through the summer of 1851 in the elections for the supreme court. Two of the incumbent judges were swept from the bench as a remorseful Missouri electorate gave a meaningless post-election tribute to Benton. Only Judge John Ryland survived, thanks to being labelled as "a Benton Democrat."[5] Even the ousted Napton and Birch had consolations of a sort. Napton lamented that the entire Benton vote went against him. However, Napton had already prepared a proslavery opinion in a case involving a slave named Dred Scott. He was spared delivering it and thereby salvaged some historical repute. Similar political defeat also relieved Birch from sitting on the appeal of his own libel action against the ousted Benton.

The new bench consisted, along with Ryland, of Hamilton R. Gamble of St. Louis, and William Scott of Clinton. All varied in their attitude toward another Missourian, Dred Scott, whose action for trespass and wrongful enslavement had already been before the court for some time and was enmeshing it then—and the entire country later—in the greatest tragedy of all, civil war. Indeed, the politicization of the court already had passed the point of no return.

4. *Jefferson Advertiser* quoted in Jack Pettison, "The Missouri Plan for the Selection of Judges," 20.
5. Don E. Fehrenbacher, *The Dred Scott Case*, 260.

THE GREAT
CONFRONTATION

10

Dred Scott

Just as there had been two Missouri Compromises, there were two *Dred Scott* lawsuits: one state, one federal. In filing his state freedom suit in 1846 before the Circuit Court of St. Louis County, Dred Scott followed a long series of litigants from Marguerite and Catiche, and his plea essentially followed theirs—that slavery involved such a basic violation of fundamental human rights that it could only exist where it was recognized, validated, and enforced by positive law, and that where slavery was not so structured its incidents fell away upon arrival on free soil with the so-called slave becoming a free man or woman. So had the great Lord Mansfield ruled in 1773 in the landmark case of *Somerset v. Stewart*.[1] Indeed, the framers of the U.S. Constitution had drawn that document to ensure that the *Somerset* doctrine should not take root on American soil. In so doing they followed the model of the Northwest Ordinance of 1787, which not only barred slavery from the northwest territory of the young republic, but also provided (contrary to *Somerset*) that a slave's escape and entry to free soil made no change in his servitude.

For a mid-nineteenth-century slave, Scott left a remarkable paper trail. Born in Virginia, he was brought to St. Louis in 1827 by his master, Captain Peter Blow. Three years later he was sold to Dr. John Emerson, an army surgeon, and went with him to sta-

1. 98 Eng. Rep. 499 (K.B. 1772).

51

tions at Rock Island Arsenal, Illinois (where slavery was forbidden by the state's constitution), and Fort Snelling, in what is now Minnesota, territory where slavery had been explicitly and positively forbidden by the Missouri Compromise. While at Fort Snelling, Scott married Harriet, a slave of Indian agent Major Talliaferro. To further complicate the legal doctrine that provided slave status as hereditary and perpetual, the Scotts had two children, one of whom had been born aboard the *Gypsy*, a steamer on the navigable waters of the United States.

Returning to St. Louis in 1837, Emerson died five years later leaving Dred Scott and his family as part of his estate. He also unwittingly immortalized his New York brother-in-law, John F. A. Sandford, by naming him coexecutor with his widow. In 1846 Scott brought his freedom suit against the two in the Circuit Court of St. Louis. He lost on a jury verdict, but a second try was successful and resulted in his freedom in January 1850.

On appeal, two novel elements distinguished Scott's suit from the earlier line of freedom litigation. The first was "reversion," a common law doctrine that took *Somerset* one step farther: even though the incidents of slavery vanished the moment a slave put his foot on free soil, a voluntary return to the territory of servitude meant that slave status reverted. Such had been asserted by Lord Stowell in 1827 in *The Slave Grace*.[2] The second was judicial review—the asserted power of the courts to declare legislation null and void, binding all branches of government and all citizens to such determination. That doctrine had slumbered unnoticed since John Marshall had voided a section of the Federal Judiciary Act in *Marbury v. Madison* (1819), and the Missouri Supreme Court uneasily followed his lead in aborting the stay law of the 1820 relief legislation. Both issues surfaced in the *Scott* lawsuit, which was litigated against the background of the rising slavery controversy in the state and the nation. A special backdrop was Missouri's 1850 spring elections for the General Assembly wherein the political future of longtime Senator Thomas Hart Benton (elected in those pre–Seventeenth Amendment days by the state legislature) became itself a litmus test of the larger slavery dispute.

The dispute carried over to the August 1851 judicial elections

2. 166 Eng. Rep. 179 (Adm. 1827).

when Napton and Birch were swept from the bench after Benton had been ousted from the Senate. It also meant that Dred Scott's appeal had to be reargued before a new panel of judges. This one consisted of William Scott, Hamilton Gamble, and John F. Ryland (the latter having been reelected). Although Judge Napton was no longer on the bench, his interminable delay with his opinion (allegedly waiting for the *Slave Grace* report) left the decision to his successors. It also left his impression on the court, for Napton had often declared his aim to overrule prior Missouri decisions that would have given Dred Scott his freedom, and he had half-persuaded his colleagues to go along. Napton was certainly un-sympathetic to freedom as a judicial ideal, asserting "it has not been the policy of this State, to favor the liberation of negroes."[3] The ousted Napton and Birch had both conferred previously with Judge Ryland of the reorganized court to push this novel thesis, which was the heart of Napton's "Jackson Resolutions." Interest-ingly, their views were not suggested in the split opinion that came down May 22, 1852; Judge Scott delivered the majority opinion with Ryland concurring.[4] Free status acquired outside Missouri's borders (whether by *Somerset* or otherwise) was essentially a matter of discretion here; Missouri adjudication was not fore-closed by any outstate decision. Hence, the Missouri Supreme Court had its choice and could make it on the ground that servile status reattached on Dred Scott's voluntary return to Missouri. Judge Scott, accordingly, quickly overruled the long line of free-dom cases, which ran back to the first volume of the reports of his own court. Times had changed, he insisted. The old decisions had been undertaken in a context of concord and harmony, but the rising antislavery agitation altered everything; "not only indi-viduals but States have been possessed with a dark and fell spirit in relation to slavery."[5] Missouri should not discourage this "dark and fell" spirit, but it should reflect that slavery was a positive good, considering the low state of Africa and the benefits result-ing from forced migration of blacks to America.

Judge Scott was scarcely a detached and neutral analyst on the

3. Charlotte v. Chouteau, 11 Mo. 193, 200 (1847).
4. Scott v. Emerson, 15 Mo. 576 (1852).
5. *Id.* at 586.

subject. Census records show him to have been a slaveholder, and his earlier opinion in *Davis v. Evans*, suggests an especial insensitivity to the cruelty of the institution.[6] In *Davis*, while denying the right of an emancipated slave mother to the child she had borne and raised, he observed that the owner who had provided her freedom was not to be penalized by expropriation of his own property. This view of the case had been stated with particular brutality by Emerson's counsel in *Dred Scott:*

> Suppose Congress should pass a law declaring that the keeping of black horses, a species of property existing in Missouri and recognized by the constitution of the United States and of Missouri "shall be and the same is hereby prohibited in the territory of Utah." The same government that passes the law through its executive department, orders an officer, who unfortunately owns a black horse that he can neither sell, lose, nor give away, to the territory of Utah, and he takes with him his said horse. (I admit that the horse, if there were horse abolitionists there, would get his freedom in Utah.)[7]

Gamble, the third judge on the court, was no overt abolitionist fanatic but if forced to choose between the peculiar institution and the Union plainly showed where his values lay: "We, here, are citizens of one nation."[8] Moreover, as the best lawyer on the court,[9] he was clearly sensitive to the claims of *stare decisis:* "While I merely glance at the reasons which might be urged in support of the present plaintiff's claim to freedom, if it were an original question. . . . I regard the questions as conclusively settled, by repeated adjudications of this court."[10]

After some delays, a final judgment against Scott was then entered in the Circuit Court of St. Louis, which should have been the end of the matter. It was not. New lawyers—and new legal theories—entered the case. Just as Napton's "Jackson Resolutions" provided a new and exacerbating dimension to freedom lit-

6. 18 Mo. 249 (1853).

7. Scott v. Emerson, 15 Mo. at 581.

8. *Id.* at 588.

9. Gamble was elected to the Missouri Supreme Court by virtual acclamation. His professional status was suggested by the sequence of cases—thirteen in thirteen years—in which he had been retained to argue before the U.S. Supreme Court.

10. Scott v. Emerson, at 589.

igation by injecting the constitutional power of Congress into the controversy, so did Dred Scott's new St. Louis lawyers resort to the United States Constitution in forging a new remedy. The lawyers were Charles La Beaume and Roswell Field, father of the future poet, Eugene Field. The pair found a second chance for Scott under Article III of the U.S. Constitution, which gave federal courts jurisdiction over controversies between citizens of different states, and *Dred Scott II* sought to exercise that jurisdiction in favor of Scott by reason of his residence in a federal territory. With the common law disabilities of women raising a question as to whether Mrs. Emerson could legally be an executor (doubtless her brother was added as insurance), suit was filed in the federal court in St. Louis against John Sandford only. Sandford was thereby assured of remembrance in American history, but his claim to fame is shaky because his participation in a landmark lawsuit has been assailed as a collusive transfer designed to give the court jurisdiction over an outstate citizen.

The federal suit was filed November 2, 1853, even though the matter was what lawyers call "res adjuciata" by the unappealed decision of the Missouri Supreme Court. Scott sued as a citizen of Missouri for a commercial wrong (not for freedom) by a citizen of New York, grounds arguably distinct from the original suit. The following spring, Sandford's lawyer filed a "plea in abatement," which challenged the right of the federal district court to hear the case at all, since as a Negro Scott was not and could not be a Missouri citizen. Scott's lawyer shrugged off the plea, insisting that the point was irrelevant. District Judge Robert Wells agreed and ordered the suit to go forward, holding that the word *citizen* had a special meaning, not just for Scott but for all suits under Article III of the U.S. Constitution. The ruling held that the word *citizen* only meant a resident of the state in question who was capable of holding property there. As a plea in abatement Sandford asserted that whatever else its merits, Scott's petition failed to state a case in law. The plea was a preemptive strike, raising the core issue at the outset. Wells should have dismissed the lawsuit, but did not.

Scott's suit asserted precisely what a free white man who had been deprived of liberty and subjected to restraints would have charged. Sandford admitted his restraint of the Scott family but insisted that his actions had been minimal and humane. The defense was irrelevant in the case of a free man, but appropriate for a slave. It inevitably threw the search back to the key question: slave or free? The "trial" took place on May 15, 1854. No witness was called, and both sides stood on an agreed statement that synopsized Dred's life and travels. The case so stated went to the jury under Judge Wells's instructions. These instructions suggested a shifting doctrine of slavery. If Scott became free under Illinois law the moment his foot touched the east bank of the Mississippi, he was free there. But sauce for the goose was sauce for the gander: it was up to Missouri law to declare his status on the return trip. This Missouri had done in *Scott v. Emerson*. Scott was a slave, and as such he could not be a citizen. Having thus reversed himself on his plea in abatement ruling, Judge Wells gave his instructions accordingly, and the jury returned a verdict for defendant Sandford.

Field appealed the judgment to the Supreme Court of the United States on behalf of Scott. For Washington counsel he enlisted Montgomery Blair, onetime St. Louis lawyer and future postmaster general of Abraham Lincoln. Blair was more than matched in his opponents, Henry Geyer (who had ousted Thomas Hart Benton from the Senate), and Reverdy Johnson of Maryland, former attorney general.

Scott's appeal sat on the Supreme Court's docket for over a year. Argument began February 11, 1856, on the two burning questions: (1) were free Negroes citizens and (2) could Congress legitimately prohibit slavery in the federal territories? Both questions were constitutional, and the text of the United States Constitution presented no clear answer. Both were entangled in contemporary political developments that had split the major parties and, beyond them, the entire republic.

The first question of free Negro citizenship had been inescapably presented in Sandford's plea in abatement, and in a sense the whole Dred Scott case hinged on the correctness of Judge Wells's refusal to dismiss that pleading at the onset. If wrong, the whole proceeding should not have been before his court at all, much less before the Supreme Court of the United States. Like the overall case, the plea in abatement issue was insoluble by conventional logic. A divided Supreme Court wrestled with it during the spring of 1856 and ordered reargument at the next term.

The case, which had previously escaped national attention, was the focus of interest when the ordered reargument began on December 15, 1856. During the four days of arguing twelve hours per day, two entangled issues of black citizenship and congressional territorial power were powerfully presented. One member of the court sought to avoid the nettle in a holding that, procedurally, Scott's servile status had been settled by the *Emerson* decision, not necessarily correctly but (by res adjudicata) finally, that Judge Wells's overruling of the plea was wrong, and that the Supreme Court had no business in proceeding further. At that point, fate forced a change in attitude of a majority of the Court who decided—perhaps spontaneously, perhaps defensively—to grasp the nettle by settling the three underlying questions once and for all: (1) was Scott a citizen, (2) did presence in Illinois and Fort Snelling make him one by automatic emancipation, and (3) was the plea in abatement properly before the United States Supreme Court?

On March 4, 1857, the new president, James Buchanan, was inaugurated and promised to "cheerfully submit" to the decision in *Dred Scott*, which had already been leaked to him by a sitting justice, whatever that decision might be.[11] Two days later, Chief Justice Taney read that decision, later appending an ex parte addition on jurisdiction. The chief justice blew Scott's appeal out of the water and back to the west bank of the Mississippi with formidable answers to the questions presented: (1) the plea in abatement was properly before the Supreme Court, which had the power to declare Judge Wells's ruling dead wrong and did so, (2) Negroes were not and could not be citizens of the United States (as a matter of the original understanding of the founding fathers), and (3) Scott was freed neither by temporary residence in Illinois, which always had had the power equal to Missouri's to declare the status of onetime slaves therein either slave or free, nor by presence at Fort Snelling where congressional prohibition of slavery violated the Fifth Amendment, namely, deprivation of property without due process of law. The chief justice added a coda while his opinion was in proof: that the second suit (*Scott v. Sandford*) was improperly before the Supreme Court since it covered the same

11. James D. Richardson, ed., *Messages and Papers of the Presidents*, 2692.

ground as the first (*Scott v. Emerson*), and that the Missouri judgment was final in view of the statute granting limited appellate jurisdiction to the federal supreme court.[12]

Taney's statement of his decision was properly dispositive, but his explanation was inflammatory and divisive. Dissenters hammered away at both in extended disagreement. More than that, the explanations caused, in one view of the matter, Taney's name to be hooted down the corridors of history. History dealt with the principals in its own way. Sandford died in a madhouse shortly after the decision. Scott did not survive his case very long and died in St. Louis on September 17, 1857. Ironically, the date was subsequently entitled Constitution Day in commemoration of the document to which he had vainly appealed.[13]

12. Scott v. Sandford, 60 U.S. 393 (1857).

13. The hostile reception to *Dred Scott* contrasts sharply with the general acceptance of the Supreme Court's ruling in the contemporary Missouri v. Iowa, 51 U.S. (10 How.) 1 (1850) where the U.S. Supreme Court settled the "Honey War," an opera bouffe in which a combination of surveyor and mapmaker errors placed Iowa's southern tier of counties in Missouri's territory. After clashes of jurisdiction (including the arrest of the eponymous beehive-hunting Missourians) and militia call-ups, suit was filed directly in the U.S. Supreme Court where the Iowa territorial claims were vindicated. See Craig Hill, "The Honey War."

11

Ouster by Truncheon

Missouri throughout its history has struggled with the seemingly insoluble issue of who shall judge as well as appoint and remove its judges. Beginning with a federal model of executive appointment and life tenure, it has moved by stages (really by convulsions) to its own Missouri Plan, which undertakes to harmonize the appointive principle with the democratic process. An intermediate way station was the adoption around the turn of the twentieth century of the initiative, referendum, and recall. Although virtually hallmarks of the gaslight Progressive era, they never achieved the high hopes held out for them for a cure for political ills of democracy.

In this process the most dramatic episode in the sequence of judicial selection and removal occurred June 14, 1865, when D. C. Coleman, adjutant general of Missouri, entered the St. Louis courthouse with a squad of St. Louis police. He interrupted oral argument in the case of *Ladd, Patrick & Co. v. Couzins*, and ordered supreme court judges Bay and Dryden to quit the bench.[1] When they declined, Coleman left the courthouse and returned with a warrant for their arrest for breach of the peace. The police then executed the warrant by hustling the two judges from their seats and bringing them before the city recorder (a kind of police court magistrate) at the police court, at Twelfth and Clark. They

1. 35 Mo. 513 (1865).

were held overnight; the next morning when no one appeared to prosecute, the charge was dismissed.

The ouster of the judges was but a flash point in a powder train that went back for over a decade. The 1857 decision of the United States Supreme Court in *Scott v. Sandford* signalled the constitutional impossibility of reconciling—via the political process— the slavery issue, western expansion, and states' rights within the original constitutional understanding. Nor was the ouster of constitutionally authorized and duly selected supreme court justices unprecedented. An earlier ouster had occurred in 1861. At that time, when war tore apart the state government, political power devolved upon a constitutional convention that had been called to consider Missouri's relationship with the Union and (as the closet Confederate Governor Claiborne Jackson had hoped) to secede therefrom.

Instead, the 1861 convention went the other way. It reaffirmed the bonds of union and undertook to govern the state itself much as the Long Parliament had done in Cromwellian England and the National Assembly in revolutionary France. Like its European prototypes, it became something of an elective despotism, dominated by fanatic ideologues intolerant of opposition. Not that the convention had aspired to power—rather power had been thrust on it by the defection to the Confederacy of Governor Jackson and a majority of the General Assembly. Of necessity, the convention constituted itself the provisional government of Missouri, selecting a governor, lieutenant governor, and secretary of state. It became the legislative authority also, and its "ordinances" were enforced as law. One such ordinance, passed in October 1861, required each civil officer to take an oath within forty days supporting the U.S. and Missouri constitutions and promising neither to take arms against federal or state (provisional) government nor to give aid or comfort to the enemies of either. In general terms, the oath was not unlike the oath that the Lincoln administration required of federal functionaries. Although the apprehension of subversion was understandable, the oath was widely regarded as an insult, and two incumbent judges of the state supreme court, William Scott and Ephraim Ewing, resigned rather than take it. Their action, plus an existing vacancy, permitted Provisional Governor Hamilton Gamble to write on a clean slate and reconstitute his old court with a trio of new judges. In January of 1862, he appointed Barton Bates, William V. N. Bay, and John D. S. Dryden as a new bench.

In 1862, the "emergency" convention adjourned sine die having provided for a gradual emancipation of Missouri-held slaves; concerns over unsettled issues were transferred to the judicial elections of 1863. The emergency convention had, partly by its own action and partly by the march of events, transferred the executive and legislative power from secessionist to militantly antislavery control. Only the judicial arm and its highest component, the state supreme court, was spared such transformation. The 1863 judicial elections accordingly became a relatively miniature arena for the bitter conflict that rent Missouri: a policy issue became a moral one and thus beyond the give-and-take of compromise. Like the abortion controversy a century later, extremes prevailed. One side saw the institution as an egregious immorality to be extirpated immediately and without compensation to those who had previously profited from it. The other side (and perhaps the majority) agreed the institution was an evil, but one to be endured for the time being and suppressed gradually with a minimum of civil unrest or financial loss.

The possibility that the state supreme court might undo the gradual emancipation of slaves (decreed by the 1861 constitution) became the core issue of the 1863 elections. The contest pitted antislavery extremists against the incumbents who were seen as potential backsliders. The incumbents, Bates, Dryden, and Bay, won—but barely. The gradualist signal came through to the constitutional convention, which on the last day of its session outlawed slavery as of 1870 and then only gradually. If the judges thought their troubles were over, they could not have been more wrong. Perhaps Bates saw what was coming, for he resigned in February 1865.

Defeat at the polls in the 1863 judicial election did not slow the radical extremists. Their response was to call yet another state convention, this one to end slavery by immediate, not gradual, emancipation and other measures "necessary to preserve in purity the elective franchise and in the promotion of the public good." The roundabout language expressed a great fear that the state supreme court or a legitimate legislature might void even the modest emancipation as planned for the future.

Just what the language entailed became clear when the convention met in St. Louis on January 6, 1865. A new constitution was drawn exterminating slavery once and for all; there was no issue here—the war was over and its triggering cause had been banished seemingly forever. Perhaps. But as long as the state supreme court remained unpurified, the possibility of a judicial veto hung over the convention's actions. To guard this flank, so to speak, the convention enacted several ordinances that could probably pass electoral muster, thereby fortifying its constitution, which would become effective July 5, 1865. The real turnabout in basic law, which the extremists saw as essential to their work, was the so-called "ousting ordinance" that turned the entire judiciary out of office on May 1, 1865, along with their clerks, sheriffs, and other functionaries.

In 1865 Governor Thomas Fletcher appointed extremist stalwarts David Wagner, Nathaniel Holmes, and Walter Lovelace to succeed Bay and Dryden on the state supreme court and to fill the seat vacated by Bates's resignation. Events then moved with the inexorability of a Greek tragedy. The new judges called a special term of the court to convene in Jefferson City on June 12, 1865. The old court chose the very day for its own special term in St. Louis. Governor Fletcher ordered the adjutant general to forewarn the old judges that they faced punishment as usurpers if they persisted in their action, and the general delivered a letter to that effect on June 13, the second day of the special term.

The stage was now set. The following day, June 14, the general and a squad of police hustled the old judges from the bench and arraigned them as common criminals before the recorder. The new court immediately got down to business with an order that the record of its predecessors in the general minute book "be expunged and for naught held."[2] It immediately heard and decided five cases pending on its predecessor's docket with the result being duly recorded in the official reports, following the decisions of the old court. The ouster was duly litigated in a series of lawsuits.[3] The results validated the ouster and were summed up in the grim maxim

---

2. A documentary history of the ouster is contained in 35 Mo. V–VIII.

3. State *ex rel.* Conrad v. Bernoudy, 40 Mo. 192 (1867); State v. Neal, 42 Mo. 119 (1868).

of Roman law, *inter arma, leges tacent,* "In time of war, the laws are silent."

The new court settled down to a period of relative stability and, despite its tainted origins, compiled a comparatively creditable record. Achievement, however, could not overcome the stain of origin which violated two fundamental jurisprudential maxims. One was participation as an accessory after the fact in what can only be described as a conspiracy to subvert the state constitution and work an electoral fraud. The second had been summed up three centuries earlier by Sir Edward Coke, *nemo debet esse judex in propria causa,* "No one should be a judge in his own case." Indeed, the magnitude of the stain on the judicial ermine, as subsequent events showed, was far greater than anything perpetrated by the Jackson Resolutions of William Napton.

The ouster ended, not with a bang but with a whimper. Judge Dryden sued Governor Fletcher in the Common Pleas Court of the City of St. Louis, but the controversy languished for years and eventually vanished as the ousted incumbents formally resigned in the war-weariness that dominated the mid-1870s.[4]

4. An even better index of the postwar forgive-and-forget mood was the ousted William V. Bay's total failure to mention the incident in his *Reminiscences of the Bench and Bar of Missouri.*

12

The Recalcitrant Priest

By 1865 the ideological ultras of Missouri's Civil War days, known in their day as the "Radicals," sensed that their time was up. The excitement of war and general attachment to the Union had given them a temporary ascendancy in Missouri, but with victory and the obvious end of slavery, the state was slowly returning to its center of gravity.[1] Hence, the Radicals were faced with a double problem: first, to ensure that slavery was extirpated, root and branch, once and for all; second, to disenfranchise not only those who had taken arms against the Union but their silent sympathizers as well. The latter sanction was to run both against the grass-roots voter and the strategically placed minority, including corporate executives, clergymen, and all civil officers.

The expulsion of the judges was part and parcel of both efforts. Not only was emancipation of slaves insulated against repeal but its opponents were rendered politically impotent. The logical

1. While it may be improper and inflammatory to refer to Missouri's 1865 constitution as the "carpetbag" constitution and its 1875 successor as the "redemption" constitution, the seamless web of American history in which antebellum Missouri was an organic part of the southern subculture suggests the accuracy of those terms, particularly in their time frame. The 1865 constitution generally resembled those imposed on the states of the defeated South by intrusive, unassimilable, unrepresentative, and alien elements, and the 1875 successor similarly reflected the general return of those areas to consensus control.

complement of the ouster ordinance was found in the "carpet-bag" constitution of 1865. The latter document had been formed by another convention that had been called by the Radicals in 1865 and was equally dominated by them. Even though called to amend the constitution of 1820, the convention followed its predecessor and acted as a legislative general assembly, ruling by ordinances that had statewide effect as unamendable law. One such ordinance summarily abolished slavery, did so forthwith by advancing the 1870 date to 1865 and granting freedom universally and unequivocally. (In point of fact, slavery had ceased to exist for several years, the slaves coming and going as they pleased with their essentially helpless but intimidating presence contributing to the growth of repression.)

The Radical legacy was found in two provisions of the 1865 constitution framed by the second convention. The first was the 1861 loyalty oath, which had driven Scott and Ewing from the bench. The second, the "iron-clad oath," was an early species of thought control, which punished those who merely sympathized with rebellion against state or nation. Indeed, it was something of a catch-22, penalizing those who opted for the Confederacy outright and those who had resisted the secessionist efforts of Governor Jackson in 1861. More than that, its reach exceeded its grasp in asserting dominion over a voter's secret thoughts in terms of sympathy with secession. Attorney Frank Blair, who had done more to save Missouri for the Union than any other man, appeared at the polls in his major general uniform and indignantly refused to be sworn.[2] George "Old Drum" Vest, longtime U.S. senator from Missouri and onetime member of the Confederate Senate (who slipped through the Radical net to reenter public life by having a Unionist law partner sign his pleadings), understandably denounced the "iron-clad" oath in pejorative terms:

> The most drastic, the most cruel, the most outrageous enactment ever known in a civilized country. No man could practice law, teach school, preach the Gospel, act as trustee, hold any office of honor, trust, or profit or vote at any election, unless he swears to never sympathize with the Confederacy or any person fighting for it. The father who had

2. See Blair v. Ridgeley, 41 Mo. 63 (1867).

given a drink of water or a crust of bread to his son who belonged to the Confederate forces was ostracized.[3]

The man who successfully brought down the iron-clad oath was a most unlikely antagonist. Despite his prominence in American legal history, Rev. John A. Cummings was and is a man of mystery. Notwithstanding the character of the Catholic church as the world's oldest and largest record-keeping organization (it is surely no accident that the word "clerical" springs from the same root as "clerk"), we are ignorant of his birthday, birthplace, or specific appearance. Nor do we know the content of the sermon that he preached September 3, 1865, which embroiled him in difficulties with the secular state.

Cummings left four monuments to his short life and brief priesthood: a terse entry in the official records of the Archdiocese of St. Louis, a belated marker at his grave site in Calvary cemetery in St. Louis (where he rests some five hundred yards from Dred Scott), and two cases in the law reports. The first involving Cummings is in the Missouri Reports, and states the core controversy: "The appellant stands convicted under sections three, six, nine and fourteen of the record article of the Constitution of this State. The ninth section, *inter alia*, declares that no persons shall 'be competent as a bishop, priest, deacon, minister, elder or other clergyman of any religious persuasion' . . . unless such person shall have first 'taken, subscribed, and filed' [the iron-clad oath]."[4] The second is in the United States Reports, reversing the Missouri judgment.

No question that Cummings had patently transgressed the letter of the law. He had *not* taken and filed the oath when he celebrated Mass and preached (on an unknown subject) to a group of Irish railroad workers at Louisiana, Missouri, on September 3,

3. William Rufus Jackson, *Missouri Democracy: A History of the Party and Its Representative Members,* 135. An example of the oath is in Judge Arnold Krekel's examination of a prospective grand juror who asserted that he had brought his dying confederate brother home for burial. "If you did that you are not qualified . . . stand aside" (North Todd Gentry, "Some Missouri Judges I Have Known," 343). However, the party did not quite have the reach of the oath of future president Andrew Johnson, who as military governor of Tennessee required amnesty applicants to swear that they had prayed for Union victory.

4. State v. Cummings, 36 Mo. 263, 271 (1865).

1865. Neither had his bishop, Peter Richard Kenrick, who stayed out of the pulpit during the Civil War lest any utterance be misconstrued. Kenrick had ordained Cummings to the Catholic priesthood in 1865 at St. John's Church in St. Louis.[5] After a brief assignment in St. Louis, Cummings went north to Louisiana in Pike County. Unquestionably he knew the consequences of not taking the oath, for the cut-off date was September 2, 1865, the day before the fateful Sunday. Nonetheless, Cummings officiated, unsworn and as scheduled. Curiously, he may well have taken the unadorned loyalty oath that had been prescribed by the 1861 convention for teachers, preachers, and officials and that had been substantially replicated in federal law. The thought control effort of the 1865 convention was something else again, and here Cummings obviously drew the line.

So did his enemies. By Monday, September 4, he was indicted in twenty minutes by the Bowling Green grand jury. On September 5, after arrest and imprisonment, he went to trial before Thomas Jefferson Fagg, circuit judge for Pike County. Cummings pleaded guilty and used his allocution to assail the constitutional oath in what the contemporary press called a religious stump speech. Luckily for him, Senator John Brooks Henderson (called "General" Henderson in contemporary reports) was in the courtroom (Cummings was fortunate in the lawyers he met quite by chance). Another lawyer spectator was Robert Alexander Campbell, son of a prominent Presbyterian minister and allegedly the only man who made a Democratic speech north of the Missouri River. Campbell and Henderson persuaded Cummings to change his plea to not guilty. Henderson, however, carried water on both shoulders in presenting the prosecution with one Pat Dyer and something he said in closing angered Campbell, the latter report-

5. Archives, Archdiocese of St. Louis. The entry is devoid of personal details, but the Reverend Donald Rau, pastor at St. Michael's Church, Portage Des Sioux, and author of "Three Cheers for Father Cummings," *Yearbook, Supreme Court Hist. Soc.* 20 (Washington: Supreme Court Historical Society, 1977), 20–30, surmises that Cummings's "bull-headed" obstinacy in refusing bail and remaining in jail is proof positive of Irish birth or at least of Irish parentage. See also William Faherty, S.J., "American Hero Anonymous: John Cummings and the Iron-Clad Oath," *St. Louis Bar Journal* 27 (Summer 1981): 56–58.

edly coming to his feet and denouncing the prosecution as a powerful and bitter persecution of the weakest victim to be found.

The outburst adds a dimension to the Cummings controversy.
Observance of the iron-clad oath was less than universal. It remained a virtual dead letter in St. Louis and similar Democratic
enclaves. But Cummings's action north of the Missouri was seen
as an effort to break the territorial equilibrium and the Radical
establishment reacted accordingly.

Cummings spent the night in the Bowling Green jail in the
company of a horse thief, two burglars, and a rapist. The next day
the actual trial was held to its predictable result. Judge Fagg fined
Cummings $500 and imposed imprisonment until the fine was
paid. The priest refused to pay the fine or allow bail to be provided. He was accordingly lodged in the Bowling Green jail while
his appeal went to the supreme court.

The Missouri Supreme Court, now reconstituted, in possession of the records of its predecessor and served by its own person-
nel, heard the case in St. Louis at the October 1865 term. The
proceedings suggest that Cummings had more in common with
Dred Scott than interment in a common resting place. Just as
Scott made his plea for freedom before judges who had no moral
problem whatsoever with the institution of slavery, so did Cummings make his argument against the oppressive oath before judges
who had taken that oath with complete equanimity.

Charles C. Whittelsey, from Connecticut, was Cummings's
lead counsel ("He was in no sense brilliant. . . . His enunciation
was too rapid and indistinct").[6] His cocounsel was Presbyterian
R. A. Campbell. They had a double-stringed bow in urging reversal
of the Cummings conviction: (1) "requiring this oath of a clergyman before he can be allowed to preach, is inconsistent with the
principles of government, as declared by the Declaration of Rights
in the . . . [Missouri] Constitution," and (2) the oath by crimi-
nalizing an action theretofore innocent was a bill of attainder and
an ex post facto law prohibited to states by the tenth section of
the first article of the federal Constitution.[7]

6. William V. Bay, *Reminiscences of the Bench and Bar of Missouri*, 421,
422.

7. *Cummings*, 36 Mo. at 263.

Judge Wagner, of the reconstitutioned court, had the smallest part in the ouster of the validly elected judges. He seemingly agreed with Cummings in the opening lines of his opinion: "Bills of attainder are justly considered odious; . . . The history of England is full of the most startling examples, where the Parliament has claimed and exercised this transcendent power." Wagner then retreated and set off a controversy that still reverberates: the provision in the state constitution "does not come within the legal meaning and sense of a bill of attainder [which] . . . is an act inflicting capital punishment." Wagner then passed to the issue of ex post facto, which a binding authority held only to apply to civil laws of a criminal nature. Here, in a subtle and nuanced insight, Wagner suggested that the constitutional constraint on the sovereign states was a question of proximity and degree—that the prescribed oath was not a criminal punishment for past conduct but a measure for future protection.[8]

In a defensive passage, every word of which upheld his own right to sit (suggestive of an uneasy conscience), Wagner denied that the oath in the 1865 constitution abrogated the religious liberty promised in its opening lines and that the inherent legislative power was to enact "general laws made for the government and to promote the welfare of the whole people."[9] Wagner then made his obeisance to the Radical establishment:

> Courts are not at liberty to declare an act of the Legislature unconstitutional and void, unless its repugnancy is clear and manifest. Respect for a co-ordinate branch of the government, the presumption that they have not transcended their powers or passed beyond the bonds of their legitimate sphere, invoke every intendment in behalf of their action. Every doubt is to be thrown in favor of the law. . . . Constitutional ordinances are high above mere legislative acts.[10]

Needless to say, the other judges concurred. His conviction affirmed, Cummings returned to Louisiana, Missouri. On the upstream riverboat he had his second fortuitous encounter, a meeting with Frank Blair, who was on his way to Hannibal to attack

8. *Id.* at 272–73. For another view, see Raoul Berger, "Bills of Attainder: A Study of Amendment by the Court," *Cornell Law Review* 63 (1978): 355.

9. *Cummings*, 36 Mo at 276.

10. *Id.* at 277.

the 1865 constitution in a speaking engagement. Cummings was not without considerable personal charm: "A very modest, gentlemanly looking little fellow," according to contemporary accounts.[11] The chance steamboat meeting brought Cummings a formidable ally. Not only was Blair a prototype of the center in kaleidoscopic Missouri politics, but, as previously noted, he was a fellow recusant as to the iron-clad oath.

In mid-September, a St. Louis circuit judge pronounced the oath unconstitutional. The judgment came in a case of a lawyer who had refused the oath and was decided on the ground unsuccessfully urged by Cummings in Pike County. Blair agreed to take the Cummings conviction before the U.S. Supreme Court. Only a person of his stature could have assembled the appeal team that he put together—his brother, former Lincoln cabinet member Montgomery Blair, Reverdy Johnson, ex-attorney general and senator from Maryland, and David Dudley Field, who had indirectly framed Missouri's reformist procedural code of 1849 and was now making his second intervention in that state. Appearing for the state were George P. Strong, an outstanding Radical lawyer and, still on both sides of the issue, Senator John B. Henderson.

Before the high tribunal, the case was argued on only the federal grounds which gave the court jurisdiction in the first place— that the oath constituted a bill of attainder and an ex post facto law, forbidden to the states by Article I, Section 10 of the U.S. Constitution. It was nice question. The distinction between a bill of attainder, which inflicted death, and legislative enactments, which imposed lesser sanctions (known as bills of pains and penalties), was well known to the men who wrote the constitution, and presumably their definition was binding, therefore, short of constitutional amendment. Nevertheless, Justice Stephen Field held that the attainder and ex post facto prohibition contextually and held that the oath penalized after the fact conduct that had been previously innocent and legal. It was therefore beyond the competence of Missouri to punish.[12]

Notably, Field's logic did not embrace freedom of religion, which at that time was not generally considered a federal right.

11. Bay, *Reminiscences*, 59 n. 7.
12. Cummings v. Missouri, 71 U.S. (4 Wall.) 277 (1866).

The closeness of the question was suggested in the wafer-thin (5-4) division of the court and also in the inability of the tribunal to come to a decision before the end of its 1866 term. Argued on March 15, 1866, the decision was announced in January 1867. Unquestionably, the nine members of the court had engaged in a titanic encounter. Unquestionably, it also took all of Field's formidable personality and will to bully his views through the Supreme Court conference in the face of the powerful historical and analytic arguments expressed in the dissent of Justice Miller.

It is a significant index of changing times that contemporary standards saw nothing amiss in Justice Field listening to (and adopting) the arguments from his own brother. The same tolerance applied to Judge Thomas J. C. Fagg of the Missouri Supreme Court who sat on the original Cummings appeal from his relative's circuit court. More than that, there had been a leak from the Supreme Court's conference room. In a speech at Macon, Missouri, on May 14, 1866, less than two months after argument and seven months before the final *Cummings* decision was announced, Frank Blair asserted: "I am here to tell you today that the Supreme Court *has* [emphasis added] decided that the Constitution [Test] Oath is invalid and void. I was told so myself by one of the Judges of the Supreme Court at Washington."[13]

Cummings's resistance to ideological thought control made him something of an instant celebrity. He was given a rousing ovation at the state convention of the resurgent Democratic party ("Three Cheers for Father Cummings").[14] His future was to be brief; shortly after his Supreme Court victory, Archbishop Kenrick transferred him from Hannibal to Indian Creek. There he became ill and returned to St. Louis where he died at St. Mary's Infirmary just ten years after his defense of religious liberty.

He was buried in the priests' lot in Calvary Cemetery where the metal cross that marked his grave site became a victim of the

13. Barclay, op. cit., "The Liberal Republican Movement in Missouri," 268 n. 31. A search of Blair's almost illegible correspondence at the University of Virginia yields no credence to the inference that Justice Stephen Field told his brother David Field, who in turn informed cocounsel Montgomery Blair who told *his* brother, Frank Blair.

14. See Rau, *Yearbook*, 20–30.

elements. In 1987, Archbishop John May, Kenrick's successor in title, provided a permanent site inscription, and Missouri's second most famous constitutional litigant rested some five hundred yards from its first—Dred Scott, whose grave there also received its marker in 1957, the centennial of *his* Supreme Court appeal.

DISCONTENTS
OF DEMOCRACY

13

Old Drum: Emblem of Reconciliation

In early October 1870, a memorable proceeding took place in the plaster-front courthouse of Warrensburg, Missouri. It was the fifth hearing over a controversy that had already been heard before both a justice of the peace and the local court of common pleas. The issue was the death of a dog, "Old Drum," allegedly shot by Dick Ferguson at the behest of one Leon Hornsby. The jury awarded the plaintiff, Charles Burden, $50, but the litigation was still not at an end: Hornsby appealed to the state supreme court on a technical point of pleading; Judge Philemon Bliss irritably sustained the jury verdict.[1]

Even more remarkable than the matter disputed were the lawyers involved. Two future Missouri senators (and ex-Confederate brigadiers) George Vest (for plaintiff) and Francis Cockrell (for defendant) found themselves on opposite sides of counsel table; one of the trial judges, J. J. Crittenden, later served as governor. Vest's partner who was also involved, John Finis Philips, later became a federal district judge and state supreme court commissioner. Most prominent of all was the slain dog "Old Drum," apotheosized for all time in Vest's closing summation:

Gentlemen of the Jury: The best friend a man has in this world may turn against him and become his enemy. His son or daughter that he

1. Burden v. Hornsby, 50 Mo. 238 (1872).

has reared with loving care may prove ungrateful. Those who are nearest and dearest to us, those whom we trust with our happiness and our good name, may become traitors to their faith. The money that a man has he may lose. It flies away from him, perhaps when he needs it most. A man's reputation may be sacrificed in a moment of ill-considered action. The people who are prone to fall on their knees to do us honor when success is with us may be the first to throw the stone of malice when failure settles its cloud upon our heads. The one absolutely unselfish friend that a man can have in this selfish world, the one that never deserts him, the one that never proves ungrateful or treacherous, is his dog. Gentlemen of the jury, a man's dog stands by him in prosperity and in poverty, in health and in sickness. He will sleep on the cold ground, where the wintry winds blow and the snow drives fierce, if only he may be near his master's side. He will kiss the hand that has no food to offer; he will lick the wounds and sores that come in encounter with the roughness of the world. He guards the sleep of his pauper master as if he were a prince. When all other friends desert he remains. When all riches take wings and reputation falls to pieces, he is as constant in his love as the sun in its journey through the heavens. If fortune drives the master forth an outcast in the world, friendless and homeless, the faithful dog asks no higher privilege than that of accompanying to guard against danger, to fight against his enemies, and when the last scene of all comes, and death takes the master in his embrace, and his body is laid away in the cold ground, no matter if all other friends pursue their way, there by his graveside will the noble dog be found, his head between his paws, his eyes sad but open in alert watchfulness, faithful and true even in death.[2]

The lawyers' alignment symbolized a new order in the war-torn state. Vest and Philips had fought on opposite sides; so had Cockrell and Crittenden. Indeed, when Vest resumed his law practice after the war he escaped the Reconstruction proscription by simply having Philips sign his pleadings.

The new concord was mirrored in a larger context. As the upheaval of the Civil War slowly abated, so did the extremist views written into Missouri's 1865 constitution. The essentially organic connection between state and nation requires that nineteenth-century state constitutions be read as part of a larger national whole. In this context, the 1865 constitution was but one of such carpetbag constitutions imposed upon the defeated slave polity

2. The context of the trial is set out at length in Walter L. Chaney, "The True Story of Old Drum," 315–16.

by an alien, intrusive, and unrepresentative minority. Similarly, the 1875 constitution was one of the "redemption" instruments. All across Dixie these followed the northern armies' withdrawal of occupation as a result of the "bargain" of 1876, whereby the dominant northern industrialism retained the presidency in exchange for permitting the defeated servile culture to deal with the problem of the black minority on its own terms. Just as the Fourteenth and Fifteenth amendments to the national constitution became dead letters (save in the service of the burgeoning finance capitalism), so did the Draconian provisions of Missouri's 1865 constitution wither because of a grass-roots passivity and statewide war-weariness that matched the national mood.

While some provisions born of the Civil War faded, some others were irreversible. The stain of chattel slavery was eradicated nationwide once and for all by the Thirteenth Amendment, which was anticipated statewide by Missouri's 1865 constitution when its draftsmen replaced their predecessors' gradual and phased program of slow emancipation with an immediate and unconditional grant of freedom.

Other problems remained, however, particularly the political status and civil rights of the freedmen. Popular sentiment was reflected in the fact that even the idealistic Radicals avoided the subject in the constitution of 1865. Instead, an entire article substantially repeated the 1820 provision, which limited suffrage to white males, and emphasized a racist bias by enfranchising white aliens who had indicated an intention of citizenship. Equally suggestive was the defeat in 1868 of a constitutional amendment enfranchising blacks. However, the political trade-off was emphasized by a forgive-and-forget amendment two years later that simultaneously eliminated the iron-clad oath of the 1865 constitution, thereby restoring civil rights to ex-Confederates, and gave the vote to the newly freed blacks. The amendment was overwhelmingly passed at the polls. War-weariness was also evident when Benjamin Gratz Brown, a "liberal" (non-Radical) Republican won the governorship in 1870, and was succeeded by Democrat Silas Woodson in 1872, who defeated the enigmatic John Brooks Henderson.

The ameliorative developments came to a head as the 1870s opened with bipartisan suggestions for yet another state constitution. It was surely time for it. Even with the Draconian provisions, the 1865 constitution essentially repeated its 1820 predecessor. That earlier document, drawn for a slave state with ten thousand inhabitants, was obviously unfit for a free and industrializing commonwealth whose population ran to well over one million. Amply authorized at the polls, the draftsmen of the new document met in Jefferson City in the spring and summer of 1875; voters ratified their handiwork the following fall.

The 1875 constitution embodied the 1870 trade-off of freedman suffrage for rebel amnesty. It also reflected the lessons of experience. Most obvious was length: longer and more complicated sections were introduced to deal with the complexities of a pluralist, democratic, and industrializing cultural climate in which the Jeffersonian simplicities of an earlier pastoral innocence were fast eroding. Disillusionment with the political process appeared in a host of checks and restraints laid upon the legislature.[3] The changes were not all idealistic. For example, registration of voters (a process with high potential for racial oppression) was downgraded from a statewide process under state authority to an essentially local concern.

The 1875 constitution left its mark on the judiciary as well. For the first time, the title "chief justice" was given constitutional recognition. Curiously, the senior presiding judge had been so designated in the first minute book but merely described as a lackluster "president" in contemporary rules of court. The court itself was expanded from three to five members with ten-year terms. The wandering of the supreme court ended with a permanent seat in Jefferson City and the establishment of an intermediate, regional tribunal of review. This was the St. Louis Court of Appeals, which relieved some of the pressure on the supreme court's docket by deciding nonconstitutional disputes of limited monetary amount. Also indicative of the necessity of economizing the state supreme court's ability to deal with its increasingly swollen docket was the elimination of a provision in the 1865 constitution authorizing advisory opinions on fundamental constitutional questions.

Finally, the changing character of the state from rural to urban

3. See Isidor Loeb, "Constitutions and Constitutional Conventions in Missouri."

was recognized in a provision granting autonomy to St. Louis through a special charter that sought to engage new problems in much the same way the establishment of a regional court of appeals did. The middecade turnabout was further reflected when Barclay Napton, who left the court during the pre–Civil War upheaval, was appointed to his old seat in 1873 and thereafter reelected to a full term. The cultural mix was complete when Missouri was represented in the United States Senate by two Confederate generals, Francis Marion Cockrell and George Graham Vest, who for three decades thereafter joined in a single cause, after having been on opposite sides of counsel table in the celebrated case of "Old Drum."

14

The Ladies, Judges, and Progressives

THE LADIES

Among closing reflections in his classic *An American Dilemma* author Gunnar Myrdal explained the choice of the indefinite article for the title of his landmark work. The reason, he said, was that the racial gap between profession and practice of an American ethos that proclaimed equality and opportunity represented only one of many social inconsistencies in which the injustices were successfully and constitutionally perpetuated both by the neurosis of race and the preconceptions of gender.[1] Nowhere was this better shown than in the actions of the Federal Reconstruction U.S. Congress and the Missouri General Assembly. Both bodies moved to enfranchise ultimately newly freed black men but were singularly unmoved to do anything about the corresponding powerlessness of women. Quite the contrary, the distinction was emphasized in the vocabulary chosen by both legislative bodies in the use of the adjective "male" in their ameliorative legislation.

Not that women of Missouri had acquiesced in the arrangement. Rather, during the intermezzo between the state's 1865 and 1875 constitutions (both of which had explicitly limited

1. Myrdal, *An American Dilemma*. Notably the Missouri Supreme Court was a leader in the movement whereby equitable intervention (via the trust) softened harsh common-law disabilities of married women. See Whitesides v. Cannon, 23 Mo. 457 (1856).

the vote to the male gender), a gathering of women met on May 8, 1867, in St. Louis's Mercantile Library and petitioned the General Assembly for the right of women to vote. Predictably, their plea lost in Jefferson City, as did their subsequent petition the next year. However, in 1869, a new element in the effort was suggested by a convention in St. Louis of the Woman Suffrage Association, a group including Elizabeth Cady Stanton, Susan B. Anthony, and St. Louis's Virginia Minor. The latter was married to her distant cousin Francis and fortuitously retained her maiden name. She had been the spearhead of the 1867 petition to the General Assembly, as had her husband—a respected lawyer and onetime clerk of the Missouri Supreme Court—who became a fervent convert to the cause of women's voting rights. A new factor appeared when the reformers changed their tactic from importuning the legislature to demands in litigation. "Failing before the Legislature," said Mrs. Minor, "we must turn to the Supreme Court."[2]

And she did, taking the first step on October 15, 1872, when she undertook to register with the St. Louis election authorities. Predictably, registrar Reece Happersett refused to enter her name in the rolls. Mrs. Minor, together with her husband (an indispensable party in view of his wife's common law disabilities), responded in December with a lawsuit in the Circuit Court of St. Louis County. They asserted that the voting sections of Missouri's 1865 constitution that limited voting to males had been nullified by the recently adopted (1868) Fourteenth Amendment to the U.S. Constitution. Joining them was John Brooks Henderson, whose close connection with the Civil War amendments to the U.S. Constitution (see chap. 10) lent his intervention as a compelling force for persuasiveness. The Fourteenth Amendment forbade any state from impairing the privileges and immunities of citizens of the United States. These, insisted the Minors and Henderson, included the right to vote. Indeed, their suit resurrected the keystone question of *Dred Scott:* who were "citizens" and what were their rights?

On February 3, 1873, the circuit court dismissed the Minors' action, and appeal was duly taken to the Missouri Supreme Court.

2. Margaret Wolf Freivogel, "St. Louisan Led Fight for Suffrage," *St. Louis Post-Dispatch*, December 13, 1987.

Before the 1873 term was out, the court unanimously sustained Happersett's refusal to register Mrs. Minor.[3] The court's logic was simplicity itself: that under the original understanding of the Constitution, admission to voting was a state matter and, aside from protection of the newly emancipated male slaves, nothing had changed.

The result of Mrs. Minor's appeal to the U.S. Supreme Court merely underscored the preemptive logic of the Missouri Supreme Court. One of Minor's lawyers on the appeal was John B. Henderson. As noted, Henderson had changed Father Cummings's plea in the Pike County court to save the constitutional issue in the iron-clad oath controversy. He had also written the Thirteenth Amendment (abolishing slavery) and had been a major protagonist of the Fifteenth (forbidding states to use slavery as a disqualification for voting but apparently permitting any other constraint). Henderson must have done his best on the brief, but he was hoist with his own petard. The argument countering his plea for Mrs. Minor asserted that if the Fourteenth Amendment conferred voting rights on all citizens, why was there the need for the Fifteenth? And such was the temper of the Supreme Court during his argument that Justice Field, author of *Cummings*, forced Mr. Minor to admit that if the Fourteenth Amendment conferred voting on all citizens (including women), logically children had that right.[4] As far as the U.S. Reports show, no counsel even appeared to argue against Mrs. Minor so obvious was the question deemed, and the Supreme Court affirmed the state tribunal.[5]

The complex of discontents exemplified in the *Minor* lawsuit was a portent of stormy times for the state supreme court in which old solutions to old problems would be tried and found wanting new ones.

THE JUDGES

Beneath the seeming tranquility of the 1875 constitution, a host of factors were converging to form a new conflict. Though superficially different, the smoldering feminist discontent of the *Minor*

3. Minor v. Happersett, 53 Mo. 58 (1873).
4. See Laura Staley, "Suffrage Movement in St. Louis during the 1870s."
5. Minor v. Happersett, 88 U.S. (21 Wal.) 162 (1874).

Virginia Minor. Courtesy of Western Historical Manuscript Collection, St. Louis, University of Missouri–St. Louis.

case was rooted in the same social disintegration that showed itself in contemporaneous structural changes in the state's judicial system. The latter development grew out of urbanization and industrialization. St. Louis had always dominated the supreme court docket, but its dominance grew with the advent of manufacturing and the carnage from the machinery of the new industrial age. Urbanization itself brought a new set of social discontents with the rise of a property-less working class, which had neither a stake in the existing order nor any hope of bettering their lot. The insolubility of current problems by the simplicities of an earlier agrarian age was judicially compounded by swollen dockets and inordinate delays. Hence, the 1875 constitution's creation of a limited, regional appellate court was a temporary palliative that set in motion a sequence of structural provisions. A second regional appellate tribunal, the Kansas City Court of Appeals, was established by an 1884 constitutional amendment, which also contemplated a like body for southwest Missouri. (The Springfield Court of Appeals, however, was not similarly established until 1910.)

An 1890 amendment to the constitution of 1875, judicially speaking, amounted to a mini constitution. The state supreme court was increased from five to seven judges and authorized to sit in two divisions, a bisection that divided the judges' labor and hopefully increased their productivity. In American terms, the divisional arrangement was something of a "first." As Judge Laurance Hyde later noted in his history of the Missouri judicial system, "Few states have had as long experience with this system as Missouri and it has made possible the most efficient use of judicial manpower." Each division's cases were required to be assigned by the whole court with the exception that division number two should have exclusive cognizance of all criminal matters. Judges were specifically designated for each division (by the dates of their election) and thereafter elected to the division in which the terms expired. Unanimous divisional opinions were final unless transferred to the court en banc on order of the division or unless a federal question was involved. In the latter instances the cause would be transferred on application of the losing party. If a judge of the division dissented, the losing party likewise had the right to have the case transferred to banc on his application: "Some cases were always assigned directly to Banc and never heard in Division. These were usually proceedings on original writs or cases of great public interest."[6]

Important as they were, the structural rearrangements were essentially peripheral and did little to arrest the flood of litigation in the industrialized state. As the first decade of the twentieth century ended, two developments argued a new order of things. One was the commissioner system, which was to become a distinctive cachet of the Missouri judicial system. The other emerged in judicial responses to the new problems of the new age: the degradation of the democratic ideal by the machine politics of the swollen cities, and the inadequacy of the common law inheritance to respond to the injustices of the new industrialism.

THE PROGRESSIVES

The consequence was a new surge of idealism and reform called "progressivism." It was exemplified on the national scene by President "Teddy" Roosevelt, and in Missouri by a crusading governor, Joseph Wingate Folk. Both sought reform, rather than revolution, through a formless political impulse to tame the dominant financial capitalism by enjoining the social obligations of property and making law more responsive to such needs.

In Missouri, the foundations of a state banking department were laid, removing deposit institutions from the jurisdiction of the secretary of state where they were treated generally the same as corporate institutions. Direct election of United States senators anticipated the Seventeenth Amendment, and a preferential primary replaced the log-rolling and secret dealing of the state political conventions. Social welfare was enforced as the school year was extended from six to eight months, and public mental health hospitals were improved. Some proposals failed simply because of their utopian nature, such as a graduated income tax to support the state university.

6. Laurance Hyde, "Historical Review of the Judicial System of Missouri," *Vernons Annotated Statutes* (1952): 1–26.

15

The Blacksmith Boss

Justin Kaplan describes turn-of-the-century St. Louis:

> In the forty years since . . . the Civil War its population had jumped
> from 160,000 to 600,000, making it the fourth largest of the nation's
> cities, but few of its agencies had kept pace with this growth. Spoils-
> men flourished in the scramble and anarchy created by an outworn city
> charter. Franchises, concessions and public properties were openly traded,
> and from time to time the citizens heard of schemes to sell the city mar-
> ket, the courthouse, and the waterworks.[1]

One inhabitant of the city was Joseph Wingate Folk. He was born
in Tennessee and died in New York, but he left such an indelible
mark on his adopted state of Missouri and its legal history that his
name cannot be omitted from any roster of outstanding governors.

Folk came to St. Louis in 1893 after he graduated from Vander-
bilt Law School. As part of the exigencies of municipal politics,
he was elected circuit attorney in 1900 with the aid of St. Louis's
real ruler, "Colonel" Edward Butler. Butler was a wealthy black-
smith who had parlayed a bipartisan control of the city stables
and the city police department into an iron command of the entire town, including the municipal electoral process.

His methods were simplicity itself and rested on the fierce loyalty of the Irish immigrants. An inherited Celtic affinity for horses

1. Justin Kaplan, *Lincoln Steffens* (New York: Simon & Schuster, 1974),
104.

made the newcomers natural recruits for employment at the city stables (in a town where all large vehicles were horse-drawn). From this entry level, the upwardly mobile naturally gravitated to the Police Department where subcultural status, economic security, a uniform, and a pension seemed a natural fulfillment of the American dream. The perverse mandate to have a policeman in every election place on election day gave Butler a tremendous influence, thanks to an on-the-spot enforcer to suppress protest over obvious voter impersonation or other fraudulent voting.

Folk and Butler were appropriate symbols of the bifurcated Missouri Democratic party, whose division into ethnic and southern wings persisted long into the twentieth century. One component was the Jefferson Club, organized by future U.S. Senator Harry Hawes and described by St. Louis literary critic William Reedy as "a crowd of young men of education and Southern sympathies and distinctive gentlemanliness"; Folk fitted the description perfectly while the other Democratic component in its ward organizations exemplified the lusty vulgarity of the immigrant subculture: "crap game, bar-tending, touting, sporting characters."[2]

The unstable alliance of the boss and the blue stocking (Folk even wore a pince-nez) showed signs of fission when Folk took office as circuit attorney in 1901 and promptly had seventeen Democratic and fifteen Republican officials indicted for election fraud. After several inconclusive passages at arms, Folk had Butler himself arrested on March 14, 1902. The episode symbolized the star-crossed careers of the two protagonists and led to one of the most fiercely criticized decisions of the Missouri Supreme Court.

The charge was attempted bribery. Its source, appropriately, was garbage—or rather the disposition of garbage—a municipal service performed under an expiring contract by the St. Louis Sanitary Company whose major stockholder was Edward Butler. St. Louis Sanitary was the only bidder for the new contract. The Board of Health had customarily—and logically—awarded such contracts. Even though its success seemed assured, Butler sought to give inevitability a helping hand by offering doctors Merrill and Chapman, members of the Board of Health, $25,000. The two doctors rejected the bribe and reported the effort to Folk.

2. Ernest Kirschten, *Catfish and Crystal*, 316.

They nonetheless awarded the contract to Sanitary (presumably for lack of an alternative), and Folk took the matter to the grand jury, who promptly indicted the boss. Convicting the boss was quite another matter. Two key witnesses jumped bail and fled to Mexico.[3]

Butler sought a change of venue, and his trial was moved to Columbia in Boone County. Folk in turn persuaded President Theodore Roosevelt to renegoitiate the U.S.-Mexico extradition treaty and bring the bail-jumping witnesses home. A swarm of reporters descended on the circuit court in Columbia, and the senior class of the University of Missouri Law School was in daily attendance. The academic ambiance of the town and the rich possibilities afforded by the university obviously impressed the defendant, who summed up his view of education: "That's a hell of a business."[4]

The overflow crowd spent much of their time on the courthouse steps, but before the autumn of 1902 was over, Folk had not only secured a conviction in Columbia but another indictment against Butler for an 1898 street-lighting bribery episode. The public apathy and cynicism that attended the widespread political corruption was shown in two very different manifestations. One was popular speech, where the saturnalia of St. Louis's municipal corruption was insouciantly labelled "boodling" and its participants "boodlers." Innocuous labels did not impress the Columbia jury, which found Butler guilty and fixed his punishment at five years' imprisonment. The other sign of public apathy came in Butler's acquittal by a Fulton jury when he was tried there on a change of venue on the 1898 street-lighting episode.

Folk's biggest defeat, however, came at the hands of the Missouri Supreme Court on the appeal of Butler's Columbia conviction. Here politics intruded for Folk, who was obviously his party's best selection to succeed Governor Dockery in the 1904 election when he undertook to participate in the argument, even though

3. St. Louis legal folklore reports that the bail jumpers consulted the distinguished Samuel Treat, former federal judge and paragon of the St. Louis bar, who in turn consulted the U.S.-Mexico extradition treaty. In a conference with his clients, Treat put the fee in a personal cash box, tugged at his muttonchop whiskers, and offered the most succinct legal advice ever: "Beat it."

4. Kirschten, *Catfish and Crystal*, 312 n. 1.

the job was the business of Attorney General Edward Crow. The appeal was argued at the October 1903 term, and the court reversed Butler's conviction in an opinion written by Judge James David Fox and suggested by Butler's attorney, Thomas J. Rowe, Sr., whose son would figure prominently in the state supreme court's history (see chap. 17).[5] Even though Butler was caught red-handed, the court held such evidence did not suffice for the bribery conviction. Instead, the charge had to rest on three elements: (1) the offer had to be made with intent to influence official judgment (this was clearly shown), (2) the offer had to be a public officer (also clearly shown), and (3) "the [action sought] must be in respect to some *question* which may by *law*" be brought before the bribee.[6] It was in the third element that attorney Rowe sprung his trap. Under the city charter of 1875, which had been authorized under autonomy granted by the 1875 "redemption" constitution, all contracts for public works had to be let by the Board of Public Works and not by the Board of Health. Here, the point that the garbage had to sanitized in the collection process became critical. Sanitization was held to be a public work equivalent to building construction. The fact that the Board of Health had been doing so for years and the strained interpretation made no difference: "The absence of power can never be supplied by construction or acquiescence."[7]

The opinion was that of a unanimous court, which ordered Butler discharged. The defeat did not slow Folk, who secured his party's nomination for governor and rolled to victory in the 1904 election.[8] He took office in 1905 as the only Democrat elected statewide and went on to become one of Missouri's great governors. However, he also took on the character of something of Iscariot in the view of the immigrant underclass who made up the

5. State v. Butler, 77 S.W. 560 (Mo. Div. 2 1903). For criticism see John T. Noonan, *Bribes* (1982), 531–51, and Kirschten, *Catfish and Crystal*, 316 n.1.

6. *Butler*, 77 S.W. at 565.

7. *Id.* at 571.

8. It also derailed the political ambitions of Supreme Court Judge James Gantt, whose quest for the Democratic nomination for governor fell between two stools at the state 1904 convention: (1) a church governance controversy where the judge was actually neutral but was suspected of being partisan and (2) the "boodler" scandal. See North T. Gentry, "Some Missouri Judges I Have Known," 342–57.

bulk of the Democratic machine's cadres and whose sensitivities on loyalty to benefactors were far more acute than concerns over bribery and good government.

Under Folk's leadership in the governor's mansion, many of the measures prized by the Progressive movement were enacted into Missouri law. He subsequently left the state to practice law in Washington and died of a heart attack in New York in 1923. He was buried in his native Tennessee where not a single Missourian of note attended his funeral. But he did lose the big one, missing his especial ambition to enter the United States Senate. Butler, however, not only avoided Folk's charges but succeeded in sending his son to Congress. He also supplied the inspiration for a "boss" character in Theodore Dreiser's novel *The Financier* (1912), which despite being set in Philadelphia obviously drew on Dreiser's observations as a St. Louis reporter. Nonetheless, Folk's supporters won the war of history in effecting an ongoing defamation of both Butler and the Missouri Supreme Court. It was summed up in the condemnation of *Post-Dispatch* staffer Orick Johns, who said a machine "was in the highest courts of the state" and also by muckraker Lincoln Steffens's assertion that "the machinery of justice broke down under the strains of boodle."[9]

9. Kirschten, *Catfish and Crystal*, 326 n.1.

16

The Rube

One area of reform that the progressivism of Joseph Folk left virtually untouched was social responsibility for the terrible carnage that the machinery of the industrial revolution inflicted on working men and women. Already a commonplace in Bismarck's Germany, Victoria's England, and a number of eastern states, the concept of workmen's compensation would not come to Missouri for a full generation after the reforming governor left the state. The basic idea was simplicity itself: an employer (or the employer's insurer) was liable for medical expenses and minimum subsistence payments as a consequence of any injury sustained by an employee in the course and as a result of the latter's employment. The employer was absolutely liable and was deprived of the classic common law defenses (contributory negligence, assumption of risk, and negligence of a fellow employee) in the event of suit. It was contemplated that the costs would be covered by insurance policies, whose premiums would in turn be passed on to the public as a cost of doing business.

The intractable nature of the problem was exemplified by the *Oglesby* litigation.[1] It all began December 11, 1892, when a Missouri Pacific freight train left Kansas City for St. Louis. When the

1. Oglesby v. Missouri Pacific R.R., 37 S.W. 829 (Mo. en banc 1899), rev'd, 51 S.W. 758 (Mo. en banc 1899); and Oglesby v. Missouri Pacific R.R. 76 S.W. 623 (Mo. en banc 1903).

train reached the Little Blue switch in Jackson County, it derailed. Car 7919 loaded with thirty thousand pounds of flour was
broken in two. There was conflicting evidence as to its prewreck
condition and the speed of the train while underway. A nineteen-
year-old brakeman, H. Rube Oglesby, lost his right leg in the train
wreck. His lawyer asked a Bates County jury for damages ("In my
humble opinion $12,000 would not be too much").[2] The jury gave
Oglesby $15,000, and the railroad appealed to the state supreme
court where the verdict was almost routinely affirmed. Then, in
an almost unprecedented move, the court granted a rehearing,
reheard the appeal, and took Oglesby's award away from him.[3]
Technically, the reversal turned on the instructions given the jury
and the nature of the proof (employer involvement) offered by
Oglesby. Practically, the controversy embodied the tensions of the
jurisprudence of the industrial age, and on it the state supreme court
split irrevocably by the narrowest of margins. One side favored
the injured employee by reason of the mere fact of accident; the
other insisted on proof. The United States Supreme Court had
previously passed on the question, resolving marginal liability for
employee injury in favor of the worker. There were dark hints
that the *Oglesby* reversal was the fruit of arcane railroad lobbying
to abort the federal precedent in Missouri controversies.

The judges who denied recovery were not hard-hearted. Rather,
they saw no difference between Oglesby and his corporate employer
and a hired man hurt on the family farm. However, had Oglesby
been a passenger rather than an employee he could have recovered.
So the great Lemuel Shaw had ruled in 1842 in *Farwell v. Boston
& Worcester Railroad*[4] by holding that when an employee took
his job he took the risk of negligent fellow employees (including,
in the *Oglesby* case, an equipment inspector). Shaw's forceful
prose and intellectual stature made the *Farwell* doctrine virtually
the law of the land.

MISSOURI LAW

However in Missouri, Valliant, Gantt, and Brace repudiated
Farwell by asserting that Oglesby's initial jury verdict should

2. *Oglesby*, 51 S.W. at 761.
3. *Id.* at 788.
4. Farwell v. Boston and Worcester, Mass. (14 Met.) 49 (1842).

be affirmed. Judge Sherwood and Chief Justice Robinson felt that it should be reversed out of hand. In the center were Burgess and Marshall, obviously uneasy about the implications of shifting accident costs to the railroads. They opted for reversal and returning the case to the trial court for further proceedings. Burgess and Marshall got their way, Sherwood and Robinson going along "in order to dispose of the case."[5] Back the case went on the 4–3 split. For his second effort, Oglesby filed a streamlined and simplified pleading in Johnson County. Again the jury found in his favor, again the railroad appealed, and again the supreme court deprived Oglesby of the fruits of his victory, again by a 4-3 vote.

The original dissenting trio of Valliant, Brace, and Gantt stood fast on the view that Oglesby had pleaded and proven a case for recovery. The prevailing quartet—Robinson, Marshall, Burgess, and Fox—insisted that he had not. The pivot of the whole controversy was whether the alleged inspection of car 7919 before it left Kansas City sufficed to insulate the railroad from liability. Even though the makeup of the four-judge majority had changed, the views of the court had not, and some cynicism was expressed over such constancy.

The replacement of Judge Thomas Sherwood by James David Fox by the Democratic state convention of 1902 was seen by the *Warrensburg Standard-Herald* as "the hoisting of a railway attorney to the Supreme Bench."[6] Moreover, the newspaper also stated the court had "at the whipcrack of the Missouri Pacific Railroad sold its soul to the corporations." In response the court brought publisher J. M. Shepherd to its bar on a charge of contempt and fined him $500.[7] The fine was levied at 10 A.M. When the news reached Warrensburg an hour later, the amount was raised by public subscription and wired to the capital. Moreover, on his return, Shepherd was greeted by a brass band and a cheering crowd at the depot.[8]

Even though he lost in the supreme court of Missouri, Rube Oglesby (thanks doubtless to the pathos of his case and the engag-

5. *Oglesby* at 786.
6. State *ex rel.* Crow v. Shepherd, 76 S.W. 79, 81–82 (1903 Mo. en banc).
7. *Id.* at 79, 89.
8. Amos Pinchot, *History of the Progressive Party*, ed. Hocker (New York: NYU Press, 1958), 205.

ing bucolity of his nickname) won in the court of public opinion. The Democratic state convention of 1904 made him a candidate for the Railroad and Warehouse Commission, the toothless predecessor of the Public Service Commission. Although losing in the general election (along with all other statewide Democratic candidates except Folk) in the antiboodler reaction, he was again nominated in 1906 and won. Thereafter, the victim of railroad transport served as the nominal master of his former employer and wore both a wing collar and the title of "The Honorable" with great dignity. More than that, Oglesby achieved a fame beyond the borders of Missouri. C. P. Connolly, an early muckraker, wrote him up in *Everybody's*, a popular magazine of that genre. Indeed, Amos Pinchot, in writing to President "Teddy" Roosevelt used the *Oglesby* case to assert that the Missouri Supreme Court "established a record which has hardly been equalled for inhumanity and partiality to corporations."[9]

Pinchot was beating a dead horse for Congress corrected the court by passing the Federal Employers Liability Act of 1908. Rube was fortunate to be elected to the Railroad Commission, a job that kept him in the public eye. His name and cases disappeared from the Missouri Reports, never again to be cited by the court that reversed his jury recovery or later by the silence with which the court reversed itself.

The reason for the eclipse was federal preemption of state remedies, as congressional action under the commerce power resolved what had become a scandal and a sanguinary one at that. Rube was lucky to get off with the loss of a leg, for in the ultrahazardous business of railroading, the average life of a brakeman was seven years. The mounting loss of life and limb prompted President Harrison—three years before Rube's accident—to call for legislation. Congress ultimately responded with the Railroad Safety Appliance Act and the Federal Employers Liability Act, the latter radically altered the classic common law defenses by which railroads had long frustrated employee claims. The state courts proved almost as intractable as the railroads, persistently permitting silent interposition of abolished defenses with the conse-

9. See C. P. Connolly, "Big Business and the Bench," *Everybody's Magazine* 29 (1912): 291, 295.

quence that Divisions 1 and 2 of the Missouri Supreme Court became nicknamed by personal injury lawyers "the Mo-Pac and the Frisco." Finally, congressional revision plus a change of heart in the United States Supreme Court (remarkably on an appeal from Missouri) signalled the dawn of a new day with new litigation for victims of the industrial revolution like Rube Oglesby.[10]

10. In Rogers v. Missouri Pacific R.R., 352 U.S. 500 (1957), the U.S. Supreme Court reversed Rogers v. Thompson, 284 S.W.2d 467 (Mo. Div. 1 1955), wherein the Missouri Supreme Court overturned a jury verdict for an injured employee by reason of an alleged admission of contributory negligence—a questionable judicial action under the constraints of the governing federal statute. Thereafter, evidence amounting virtually to a suicidal intent was required to annul an employee recovery.

17

Monopoly

The Missouri Supreme Court's encounter with the problem of monopoly was far from its finest hour. Nonetheless, in defense of the court it might be said that the episode exemplified the classic, conservative judicial reflex to the stimulus of an unprecedented problem. In any event, the court's unimaginative response mirrored that of both the country and the U.S. Supreme Court.

Curiously, it was the Missouri legislature that had led Congress in the area. Borrowing from populist Kansas, the General Assembly passed its own antimonopoly statute a year before Congress followed suit and enacted the 1890 Sherman Anti-Trust Act.[1] The Missouri law forbade pools, trusts, and conspiracies to fix prices or monopolize sales under pain of fine, imprisonment, and forfeiture of corporate charter. A special provision required that corporate officers file annually an affidavit that their firms had not violated the law.

Enforcement was primarily vested in the Secretary of State Alexander Lesueur. The law got off to a bad start. The affidavit provision was widely ignored by corporations and St. Louis circuit attorney Ashley C. Clover moved to bring noncomplying violators before a grand jury. In addition, Attorney General Crow sued the noncomplying Simmons Hardware Company in an original action in the state supreme court. In an opinion that sounded

1. 1889 Mo. Laws 96–98.

like a brief of the still unborn American Civil Liberties Union, the court declared the 1889 law unconstitutional because of the affidavit's coerced self-incrimination. The court did not deal with the company's other claim (made with a straight face) that the law violated the contracts clause of the U.S. Constitution by impairing price-fixing agreements.[2]

Such was the popular outcry against monopoly oppression that the General Assembly promptly passed a revised version of the statute.[3] The antitrust affidavit was retained but enforcement transferred to the attorney general, thereby requiring that a court proceeding precede a charter forfeiture rather than a unilateral bureaucratic action.

THE TERMINAL RAILROAD ASSOCIATION

The statute was not relevant to the Missouri Supreme Court's next brush with monopoly. The confrontation involved the Terminal Railroad Association, itself an almost classic example of technological innovation and entrepreneurial rapacity characteristic of the Gilded Age of American capitalism. The association, put together by fifteen railroads with a helpful nudge from the J. P. Morgan interests, integrated two bridges across the Mississippi River (the Eads Bridge, an engineering marvel of its day, and the Merchants' Bridge) with Union Station and the Terminal Railroad into a depot and switching complex. It then proceeded to milk St. Louis interests by way of a "bridge arbitrary fee," which was an extortionate levy on east-to-west traffic across the river. Attorney General Edward Coke Crow moved against the association by invoking a provision of the 1875 constitution that forbade the combination of parallel or competing railroads.[4] He lost in the Missouri Supreme Court by a 4–3 vote. Writing for the majority, Judge Valliant (for himself and Judges Brace, Burgess and Fox) suggested that the draftsmen of the 1875 constitution did not know what they were doing: "We must conclude either that a system of terminal railroad appliances . . . had not been conceived by the

2. State *ex rel.* Attorney General v. Simmons Hardware Co., 18 S.W. 1125 (Mo. Div. 1 1892).
3. 1891 Mo. Laws 186–89.
4. Mo. Const., art. XII, 17 (1875).

members of the convention, or else that they did not understand that they were affecting that class of public utilities when they adopted the clause now under consideration."[5] Judges Robinson, Gantt, and Marshall disagreed, insisting that the plain words "parallel or competing" meant what they said.

As in prior shuttlecock exchanges between state and federal governments, and particularly the supervention shown in the *Oglesby* case, the deleterious social effects of the Missouri judgment were offset by federal action. Almost as soon as the ink had dried on the Missouri judgment in 1904, the U.S. attorney in St. Louis, under the direction of the U.S. attorney general, sued the association charging a violation of the Federal Anti-Trust Act. The tortuous and extended litigation lasted until March 2, 1914, when a decree was entered as ordered and upheld by the U.S. Supreme Court. The resolution of the case was not a clean-cut victory for either side. Nonetheless, the decree abolished the "arbitrary."[6] So, the final chapter of the Terminal Railroad Association controversy did show that the courts were learning.

To be sure both state and federal courts were learners but slow ones. The *Simmons Hardware* case in Missouri was more than paralleled in the *E. C. Knight* proceeding in the U.S. Supreme Court.[7] In *Knight,* the court declared that a monopoly of sugar refinery facilities did not violate the Sherman Act, just as its Missouri counterpart pounced on a questionable marginal item to invalidate an entire statute. Both decisions were symbols of cultural lag—the inability of judges schooled in Jeffersonian simplicities to engage the complexities of the industrial age.

STANDARD OIL

An archetypical example of the learning process was involved in the taming at both state and federal levels of the biggest, most complex, and most formidable of the monopolies—Standard Oil. In September 1904, Standard Oil began to build a ten-thousand-barrel refinery at Sugar Hill near Kansas City, Missouri. The installation could well have been an anticipatory ploy to the ouster

5. State v. Terminal Ass'n of St. Louis, 81 S.W. 395, 397 (Mo. en banc 1904).
6. See Terminal R.R. Assn. v. 266 U.S. 17, 25 (1924).
7. United States v. E.C. Knight Co., 156 U.S. 1 (1895).

suit commenced by Attorney General Herbert Hadley against Standard Oil the following June.

The report of a special commissioner found that Standard had indeed violated the Missouri antimonopoly statute by suppressing competition, dividing state territory, and fixing prices. Hadley argued the case forcefully when the report came before the court en banc, as he flayed the trust and called the case the most important since *Dred Scott*. His oratory carried him to the governorship. In December 1908, a formal decree of ouster was entered, and Hadley moved up to the governor's chair. Overruling *Simmons Hardware*, the constitutionality of the antitrust affidavit was specifically upheld and the law generally sustained.

Standard was not finished, however. The threat of closure of the Sugar Hill refinery moved the General Assembly to vacate the court's judgment of ouster, an enactment vetoed by Governor Elliott Major (who, like Hadley, had ridden the *Standard Oil* litigation from the attorney general's office to the governorship) with the buck stopping once again at the Missouri Supreme Court. The court, on appropriate application, modified its ouster decree to permit Standard Oil to stay in the state upon assurances of law-abiding behavior.[8]

The development in the law-favoring regulation over extermination reflected the national moral attitude. Herbert Hadley himself radically modified his trust-busting rhetoric.[9] So did the U.S. Supreme Court, which adopted a "rule of reason" in lieu of Sherman Act sanctions when Standard Oil stood before its bar.[10] Most representative of all was the trust-busting "Teddy" Roosevelt with his big stick and equally big mouth. Roosevelt never really modified his talk against monopoly as a hideous monster. Indeed, a critical journalist (Peter Finley Dunne) summed up his promise as a pledge to trample the hideous monster monopolies underfoot, but his subdued actions showed he would do so slowly.

8. State v. Standard Oil Co., 116 S.W. 902, 1060 (Mo. en banc 1909), *aff'd*, 224 U.S. 270 (1912).

9. See Marshall Hier, "Attorney General Hadley and the Oil Trust," *St. Louis Bar Journal* 35 (1989): 50–52.

10. Standard Oil v. United States, 221 U.S. 1 (1911).

18

The Commissioners

The report in the *Standard Oil* case, doubtless the longest one in the volumes of the supreme court, ran to a monstrous 507 pages. The record was similarly elongated. In like manner the two *Oglesby* lawsuits (thanks to the persisting 4–3 division of the court) involved a double treatment with opinions and massive layers of testimony, documents, and exhibits. Little wonder that Rube Oglesby had to wait eleven years from the time his leg was severed until his complaint was finally resolved.

New times meant new problems. New problems meant searches for new solutions as the quest moved into the tentative probing and case-by-case resolution by the common law, adversary process. Meanwhile, the state supreme court fell behind steadily. Public concern was reflected in a legislative inquiry of 1883 that found the court had over one thousand cases on its docket and that the number was growing as new filings exceeded dispositions.

The reasons were not hard to find: Missouri had changed. The ten-thousand-odd people who brought their quarrels to Judge Matthias McGirk and the early court now numbered over a million. The quarrels were different too—injuries that went unnoticed and overlooked in a rude frontier culture were resented and remembered in the emerging class hatreds of an industrial age. Finally, there was the misplaced consequence of the Jacksonian ideal. Appeal from an adverse trial result, considered indispensable to due process and as such available as a matter of right, took its own special toll. A letter from one Jay Torrey to the *St. Louis Globe Democrat* of December 11, 1880, summed up the resulting snarl:

> The Supreme Court of Missouri is hopelessly behind in its docket. If no new cases were appealed thereto it is estimated that it would take a bench of five members, the number now sitting, at least three years to decide all cases before it. Since the Court is so far behind there is a very great inducement for a defeated litigant to appeal his case thereto in all cases. . . . Since in addition to the possibility of ultimate success there is an assurance that he will not have to respond to the judgment for at least three years. This being the case, there is a very large percent of cases appealed to the Supreme Court now than there would be if it was up with its docket.

An immediate solution seemed obvious. First, the incoming flood had to be checked, or at least, reduced. Second, resources for adjudication had to be increased. And third, somehow, the adjudicators had to be given more time for analysis and reflection. Providing divisions and increasing the judges perversely exacerbated the problem by increasing (and disproportionately so) the time required for conferences and personal interchanges.

In 1883, however, the axe was laid to the root in a brilliant legislative maneuver that provided the cachet of Missouri's judicial system and an ongoing instrument of reform. It was borrowed from Nebraska (under the hallmark of Roscoe Pound), although the use of a special hearing officer by a court of review was a virtual common law commonplace. This was the institution of "commissioners." These were appointed by the court, not the executive, and consisted of three persons for a two-year term to whom cases might be referred by the court with agreement of the litigants. The reports of the commissioners on such cases might be approved, revised, or rejected by the court, but if approved became judgments of the court itself.

The advantages were manifest. The selection process neatly bypassed the corrupt convention system and ensured the choice of incumbents of judicial temperament by the group best qualified to appraise that elusive and indefinable characteristic—the supreme court itself. Next was the effect on judicial logistics to permit a relatively speedy disposition of the docket assigning the "easy" cases to the judges of the court on a rotation basis but extracting and assigning to a commissioner a particular complex and massive controversy that required close and insightful reading and subsequent reflection without the intellectual press of other concerns.

Almost before the ink dried on the governor's signature of the enabling act, the court moved to make its appointments. Charles Winslow (Jefferson City), John Finis Philips (Kansas City), and Alexander Martin (St. Louis) were selected. The group represented not only a nice sectional balance within the state but a blend of professional background and experience. Winslow, a native New Englander, had been a telegrapher, a marble cutter, and a country newspaperman before becoming engrossed in the law. Thereafter, he had served as deputy circuit clerk (Keytesville) and judge of the Chariton County court of common pleas. Practicing in both St. Louis and Carrollton, he was a frequent advocate at the supreme court's bar before his appointment. He died of consumption within a year of his succession. His eulogy stated that he was perhaps better known to the bench and bar of this state than the public generally but nonetheless was distinguished in the labors of his position. Winslow's eulogist was his coappointee, Alexander Martin, an ex-Mississippian and Harvard Law School alumnus. The latter had taught at the proprietary St. Louis Law School for nine years and had been the Missouri correspondent for the *American Law Register* of Philadelphia even longer. Following his years as commissioner, Martin served as the second dean of the University of Missouri Law School. Kansas City's John Finis Philips was the only native Missourian in the trio. Born in Boone County, he had attended the University of Missouri and Centre College in Danville, Kentucky. Philips, a four-term congressman prior to his appointment, made Missouri legal history when he temporarily left the bench under leave of absence to defend the indigent outlaw Frank James on a charge of train robbery. James had actually surrendered to Governor Thomas Crittenden on the assurance of Philips's services. That defense was capped by a moving plea that produced an acquittal and provided James thereafter with a docile and law-abiding life.

The state supreme court referred 150 cases upon their appointment to the commissioners and a total of 468 cases during the initial two-year term. The first fruits of the experiment came in *The Board of President and Directors of the St. Louis Public Schools v. Wood* delivered at the April 1883 term by Commissioner Martin. It was a simple, relatively straightforward question, which differed radically from the massive cases subsequently referred, such as *Leggett v. Missouri State Life Ins. Co.* whose transcript on appeal contained eighteen thousand pages and occupied ten feet of shelving.[1]

The commissioner experiment proved its worth in a double development. In immediate terms, the first three appointees earned their salt in eliminating the backlog that had brought them to the bench. The root causes, however, would not yield to a temporary palliative. Moreover, a mistaken perception of the effect of an 1884 constitutional amendment, which added the Kansas City Court of Appeals as a second appellate tribunal to the state's judicial mechanism, only exacerbated the problem and guaranteed its return. Unquestionably the massive turn-of-the-century antitrust cases where the court used specially designated circuit court judges as de facto commissioners more than vindicated the value of the office and compelled institutional reestablishment.

The solution lay not in more judges and more courts but in a precisely focused instrument aimed at the controls within the supreme court's docket itself. A frank confession of error came in 1911 when the office of commissioner was reinstituted.[2] Now, four commissioners were provided with qualifications—the same as for the court itself—and subject to the condition of bipartisanship. Another insulation from the shifting winds of electoral majorities continued in the provision for appointment by the court itself.

The commissioners were sui generis; always scrupulously saluted as "Judge" and "Your Honor," they were something less than that. Paul Barrett, who served longest of them, sometimes in gentle deprecation referred to himself as "a lowly commissioner."[3] They did not sit with the court on applications for extraordinary writs, and on rare en banc occasions they were placed at

1. 77 Mo. 197 (1883), 342 S.W.2d 833 (Mo. en banc 1960).
2. 1911 Mo. Laws 190–92.
3. Personal recollection of the author.

a long table in front of the regular bench. Nonetheless, they provided the distinctive cachet of the court as a judicial rather than a political tribunal. Indeed, they provided a matrix of incumbents (such as Laurance Hyde) unavailable by the political process. Their work fortified the stability and continuity of the work of the court and, more important, did so for nearly a century until abolished, perhaps too hastily, by a 1976 constitutional amendment and subsequent legislation.

19

The Home

The court had been wandering since its very beginning. Pursuant to the 1820 constitution, the first General Assembly divided the new state into four circuits, and the newly created state supreme court was ordered to sit twice per year in St. Charles, St. Louis, Franklin, and Jackson.[1] The sessions were enjoined quite irrespective of the amount of pending business or the state of the docket. Consequently, in the outstate backwaters the required sessions of the supreme court were perfunctoriness itself: "Met at 20 minutes after 6 p.m.," ran an early entry in Jackson, "[and] adjourned to meet next term."[2] Theoretically, the system kept the high court in touch with the people, but in fact the system was wretched: it made couriers out of aging men, it enormously elongated the process of deciding, and the hazards of frontier traveling conditions presented a positive danger to the judges involved in it.

As settlement and urbanization crept westward, the legislature adjusted the circuit boundaries to accommodate the flow and concentration of litigation. Fayette and Bowling Green were early added to the list of session sites. In 1843, the General Assembly set Jefferson City as a court site. However, the sheer logis-

1. 1820 Mo. Laws 273.
2. Entry of June 18, 1821, General Minute Book 1815–1826, Missouri Historical Society, St. Louis, Missouri.

tics of the caseload were not to be denied; the eastern Missouri component was specially recognized in an 1849 requirement for two annual sessions in St. Louis; a western analog emerged in 1864 with a like provision for St. Joseph. The situation persisted until the 1870s with an occasional term of court being held in Hannibal.

Finally, in 1872 Governor B. Gratz Brown proposed (along with a recommendation to increase the court from three to five) that the peripatetic status of the court end and that a fixed location be assigned for its sessions. Ultimately adopted in the constitution of 1875, the provisions were part of a larger work-cutting whole that included creation of the St. Louis Court of Appeals and elimination of advisory opinions.[3]

Suitably assured of a permanent site, the court moved into the state capitol for its 1877 term. The move was, of course, intrusive upon existing interests, and the new quarters were (perhaps by grudging acquiescence) cramped and unsuitable. The General Assembly responded with a $17,000 building appropriation.[4] Constructed with convict labor from the nearby state penitentiary, a building was placed on the southeast corner of the grounds of the state capitol. Built of the same type of material used in the capitol, the home of the supreme court bore a distinct resemblance to the latter structure.

The successor building was composed of brick and erected in the French Renaissance classical style. The style had been popularized at the St. Louis World's Fair of 1904, and the event was reflected after a fashion when the inadequacies of the original structure became apparent in the day-to-day operation of the court. There was an unspent surplus of $190,000 in the appropriation for Missouri's participation in the fair; this surplus provided the wherewithal for the new structure.

There was another strand in the tapestry that linked the new building, the famous World's Fair, and the life-style of the members of the Missouri Supreme Court. The general counsel of the Louisiana Purchase Exposition Company was Franklin Ferris of

3. See Isidor Loeb, "Constitutions and Constitutional Conventions in Missouri," 189–246.
4. See Joseph Summers, "A Home for the Supreme Court," *Missouri Supreme Court Historical Bulletin* 1 (Winter 1980): 8–12.

Current home of the supreme court. Courtesy of The Supreme Court
of Missouri.

the St. Louis bar, and unquestionably it was his knowledge of the
labyrinthine financial infrastructure of that gigantic undertaking
which afforded the unexpended appropriation for the supreme
court's permanent home. In a sense, Ferris was making provision
for an unforeseen future. The new building had chambers for the
members of the court, which included sleeping accommodations
as well as working quarters. Ferris became well acquainted with
the sleeping accommodations. A Democrat, he was appointed to
the court by Republican Governor Hadley in 1910 for an unex-
pired term of two years. Mrs. Ferris did not accompany him to
Jefferson City but instead remained in their St. Louis home. After
two years in the monastic environment of the building he helped
to provide, Judge Ferris chose not to run for a full term but returned to St. Louis when his interim appointment ended in 1912.[5]

5. Author's interview, Franklin Ferris II, October 16, 1988.

THE MODERN
COURT

20

Missouri *Jarndyce*

In January 1922, Missouri Insurance Superintendent Ben Hyde ordered a 10 percent reduction in fire insurance rates. He did so pursuant to a vaguely worded late-nineteenth-century statute prescribing "fair" rates and authorizing equally imprecise procedures for obtaining them. Predictably, the insurers resisted.

Insurance premiums had a long and tangled history in Missouri. Customarily the insurers pooled their experience to derive their charges, and the action came close to violating Missouri's pre–Sherman Act statute denouncing pools, trusts, and monopolies. Indeed, at the turn of the century ninety-five insurers had been ousted (temporarily) from doing business in the state by the supreme court for violation of Missouri's "little" antitrust act.[1]

In the later controversy Hyde did not know what he was starting. Just as a pebble tossed down a mountainside may well cause an avalanche, at least four consequences followed the superintendent's action. First was the most extended litigation in Missouri history,[2] and with that litigation came three interrelated results:

1. State *ex rel.* Crow v. Firemen's Fund Ins. Co., 52 S.W. 595 (Mo. en banc 1899).
2. In terms of sheer longevity, the Missouri palm must go to the Mullanphy will litigation (leaving a benefaction to "poor immigrants coming to St. Louis, bona fide, to settle in the West"), which went to state supreme court five times: St. Louis v. McAllister, 257 S.W. 425 (Mo. en banc 1923), until Commissioner Hyde resolved it in Thatcher v. Lewis, 76 S.W.2d 677 (Mo. Div. 1 1934); St. Louis

the bitterest judicial primary ever, the downfall and imprison-ment of "Boss" Tom Pendergast, and the most savage public feud within the Missouri Supreme Court since it first sat in 1821. More-over, the case bifurcated, being litigated on both sides of the state when after Hyde's ordered reduction the insurers unilaterally raised their rates, impounded the increase, and undertook to de-fend their action in the Kansas City federal courts.

The extended wrangle over a fair premium caused the contro-versy to be a perennial within the state's judicial machinery and provoked a number of side trips to federal tribunals including two to the United States Supreme Court itself. Two decades after Hyde's action, Commissioner Paul Barrett wearily summed up the ex-tended litigation:

> As far as we have been able to discover, this is the twenty-first case in the Missouri courts involving the fire insurance rate litigation which began in 1922. . . .
>
> It has been thought that each case would be the last and absolutely exhaustive of the possibilities of further . . . litigation, but as time passes . . . novel and conflicting interpretations are placed on the former opinions of this court and every sentence is seized on as de-claring some rule of law determinative of the new issue.[3]

In content and character, the fire insurance rate litigation resem-bled nothing quite so much as the interminable *Jarndyce v. Jarn-dyce*, which dragged on for years in Dickens's *Bleak House:* "This scarecrow of a suit, has, in the course of time become so complicated, that no man alive knows what it means. The par-ties to it understand it the least, but it has been observed that no two . . . lawyers can talk about it for five minutes, without com-ing to a total disagreement as to all the premises."[4]

Unlike *Jarndyce*, the Missouri rate litigation took place in a

---

v. McAllister, 218 S.W. 312 (Mo. en banc 1920); St. Louis v. Crow, 71 S.W. 132 (Mo. Div. 1 1902); St. Louis v. Wenneker, 47 S.W. 105 (1898); Chamber v. St. Louis, 29 Mo. 543 (1860). However, in sheer complexity it cannot compare with the insurance rate cases, which run from Aetna Ins. Co. v. Hyde, 285 S.W. 65 (Mo. en banc 1926) to Barker v. Leggett, 295 S.W.2d 836 (Mo. en banc 1956) with specific items noted at 6 *infra*.

3. Lucas v. Central Missouri Trust, 166 S.W.2d 1053, 1055–56 (Mo. Div. 2 1942).

4. Charles Dickens, *Bleak House* (New York: Hurd and Hough, 1871), 15.

broader legal context and involved both state and federal governments in an effort to deal with the problems of fair insurance rates.
The rate-making activity was frequently seen as illegal price fixing, and shortly after World War II broke out the insurance industry was taken to the U.S. Supreme Court by the Anti-Trust Division of the Department of Justice.[5] Moreover, the almost cynical
manipulation of pricing under the cloak of scientific objectivity
was particularly infuriating.

The litigation began almost simultaneously with the 10 percent reduction order when, pursuant to the statute, the insurers
went to court to contest it. Generally, following the statute, they
collected the old rate while litigation was pending but agreed to
repay the 10 percent increase to the policyholders should they lose.
They did lose, notwithstanding a fruitless appeal to Washington,
and repaid the overcharge to some but not all of the policyholders.[6] The incumbent superintendent of insurance (by this time
the office had turned over four times since Hyde's original order)
then sued to force disbursement of the balance. The Circuit Court
of Cole County granted his request, ordering the balance paid into
its registry and appointed masters to determine specific amounts
owed. As records were submitted, the court ordered determined
sums to be deposited in the Central Missouri Trust Company of
Jefferson City in the court's name to be disbursed against specific
order. To assist it, the court appointed two veteran Democratic
politicians, Lewis Hord Cook and H. P. Lauf, as custodians and
allowed them counsel. Their expenses were to be paid from the
impounded funds.

Concurrently, parallel litigation went forward when the insur-

5. United States v. Southeastern Underwriters Ass'n., 322 U.S. 533 (1944).
6. Chronologically the 10 percent cases are: Aetna Ins. Co. v. Hyde, 285
S.W. 65 (Mo. en banc 1926); State v. Westhues, 290 S.W. 65 (Mo. en banc 1926);
Aetna Ins. Co. v. Hyde, 34 F. 2d 185 (W.D. Mo. 1929), *affirmed by* National Fire
Ins. Co. v. Thompson, 281 U.S. 331 (1930); Aetna Ins. Co. v. Hyde, 34 S.W. 2d 85
(Mo. en banc 1930); State *ex rel.* Abeille Fire Ins. Co. v. Sevier, 73 S.W. 2d 361
(Mo. en banc 1934); Aetna Ins. Co. v. O'Malley, 118 S.W. 2d 3 (Mo. en banc
1938); Aetna Ins. Co. v. O'Malley, 124 S.W. 2d 1164 (Mo. en banc 1939); State v.
Weatherby, 129 S.W. 2d 887 (Mo. Div. 1 1939); State *ex rel.* Robertson v. Sevier,
132 S.W. 2d 961 (Mo. en banc 1939); Lucas v. Central Missouri Trust Co., 162
S.W. 2d 569 (Mo. en banc 1942); Barker v. Legget, 295 S.W. 2d 836 (Mo. en banc
1956).

ers unilaterally raised their rates by a challenged 16 $^2/_3$ percent.[7] Matters came to a head in 1938. The Missouri Supreme Court had been evenly divided on the legitimacy of the custodian appointments and their expenses. The deadlock was broken by the appointment of James Marsh Douglas to the court succeeding Judge John Caskie Collett. On arrival in Jefferson City Douglas joined Judges Gantt, Hays, and Frank to void the order for the custodian appointments and their expenses on the basis of a straightforward reading of the statute. When Douglas filed for re-election in 1938 to a full term he triggered the bitterest judicial primary in Missouri history.

In something of a sideshow, some representatives of the insurance industry undertook to bribe the insurance superintendent through an emolument to his master, Boss Pendergast. Each strand in the tangled skein deserves separate examination but taken together the bizarre tapestry forms a remarkable component of the remarkable history of a remarkable court.

7. Chronologically the 16 $^2/_3$ percent cases are: State *ex rel.* North British & Mercantile Ins. Co. v. Thompson, 52 S.W. 2d 472 (Mo. en banc 1932); State v. American Colony Ins. Co., 80 S.W. 2d 876 (Mo. en banc 1934); State *ex rel.* Thompson v. Sevier, 80 S.W. 2d 893 (Mo. en banc 1934); State *ex rel.* Pennsylvania Fire Ins. Co. v. Sevier, 102 S.W. 2d 882 (Mo. en banc 1937); American Constitution Fire Assurance Co. v. O'Malley, 113 S.W. 2d 795 (Mo. en banc 1938); State *ex rel.* Robertson v. Sevier, 115 S.W. 2d 810 (Mo. en banc 1938); American Constitution Fire Assurance Co. v. Robertson, 120 S.W. 2d 43 (Mo. en banc 1938); State *ex rel.* v. Carwood Realty Co. v. Dinwiddie, 122 S.W. 2d 912 (Mo. en banc 1938); State *ex rel.* Lucas v. Blair, 144 S.W. 2d 106 (Mo. en banc 1940); Lucas v. Central Missouri Trust Co., 116 S.W. 2d 1053 (Mo. Div. 2 1942).

21

The Bitter Primary

Alongside the Missouri insurance rate controversy, *Jarndyce v. Jarndyce* was simplicity itself. *Jarndyce* was and remained a single lawsuit, while both federal and state courts got involved in the rate controversy. The Missouri case had two components that were intimately related for the ambiguous regulatory statute lay at the root of both, and the powers and jurisdiction of insurance superintendent and court were likewise at issue.

Indeed, the first 10 percent reduction (1922) and the second $16\,^2/_3$ percent increase (1929) controversies were almost Siamese twins; for the second suit a case could be made along the following lines: If the 1922 reduction forced the insurers to sell their product below cost, the result was a confiscation of their property just as surely as if the General Assembly had formally expropriated it. Hence, the insurer's response seven years later could be seen as both justified self-defense and elementary survival. That response came in December 1929 when the fire insurance companies doing business in the state raised their (still unreduced) rates $16\,^2/_3$ percent that recaptured the lost ground and more. That action divided the long rate controversy into two components, each with its galaxy of lawsuits and appeals: the "10% rate reduction cases" and "the $16\,^2/_3$% rate increase cases."[1]

1. See Lucas v. Central Mo. Trust Co., 166 S.W.2d 1053, 1055 (Mo. Div. 2 1942).

The superintendent of insurance refused to approve the 1929 rate hike, and the insurers sued to void his disapproval. The federal district court for western Missouri then stayed the superintendent's disapproval and ordered the collected rate increase impounded. It was deposited by the superintendent (in a doubtful addendum) in two Jefferson City banks, the Exchange National Bank and the Central Missouri Trust Company. The fund mounted. Most proceeds were distributed to policyholders but a substantial residue remained. The superintendent of insurance moved to force a total disbursement. The insurers countered to restrain his action. Out of the welter of litigation a compromise emerged whereby the superintendent and the insurers agreed that the residual fund would be divided: 20 percent to policyholders and 80 percent to insurers *and* for expenses. Ninety percent of the rate increase was validated and made permanent. A federal decree was entered to that effect and distribution commenced.

Concurrently, the core issue—who was legal custodian of the disputed premiums and who held the residual interest—advanced to the supreme court where it presented the newly appointed James Marsh Douglas with an upsetting dilemma. Douglas came to a divided court. Three judges favored the compromise; the others felt it was unlawful. The latter group believed that *all* the money should go to the policyholders. Douglas agreed with them.

Douglas's instinct was sound. How the compromise came to pass is a separate and subsequent story. On the division of the impounded funds, Douglas tipped the balance on an equally divided court, holding the insurance superintendent as the sole custodian of the impounded funds, which belonged in toto to the overcharged policyholders. Douglas, a St. Louis circuit judge, had been appointed to the state supreme court by Governor Stark in early 1937 and had routinely filed for a full term at the 1938 election.[2]

Generally, judicial elections were pretty tame stuff. There were exceptions. The *St. Louis Republic* pronounced the supreme court nomination awarded at the 1888 Democratic judicial convention (separate conventions were used to nominate judges) as "one of the most exciting and hotly contested fights ever known

2. Clarence Miller, *Shepherd Barclay.*

in the political history of Missouri."[3] Sometimes contests were selective, as when the *Warrensburg Standard-Herald* reported in 1902 that the court had been reconstituted to please the Missouri Pacific Railroad.

But post-*Oglesby*, among hard-bitten political professionals, the general attitude toward judicial aspiration was expressed by Kansas City boss, Thomas J. Pendergast. It was disclosed in an oft-told tale of Judge Ernest Tipton, who solicited Pendergast's support in undertaking to seek election to the Missouri Supreme Court:

> TJP: What the hell do you want to do a goddamn thing like that for? You won't have any patronage and you will be buried.
> ET: Well, that's what I want.
> TJP: Well, I hate to see you do it, but if that is what you want, ok.[4]

Notwithstanding Pendergast's profane disparagement, a pilgrimage to the Jackson County Democratic Club at 1908 Main Street in Kansas City (where the boss kept regular office hours to interview aspirants to all offices, judicial and otherwise) became standard practice for prospective candidates in Missouri political selection. Indeed, virtually every aspirant undertook it as a matter of course. As Judge Merrill Otis put it:

> His throne room was a small monastic-like cubicle on the second floor of a two-story building, well removed from the business center of the city. "1908 Main Street" was synonymous with power, it was the local Mecca of the faithful. To this Mecca came he who would be governor, he who would be senator, he who would be judge, and he who was content to be only a keeper of the pound. Thither came alike great and little, craving audience and favors. They "beat a pathway" to the Boss's door, as Emerson said men would beat a pathway to the door of him who could make a better mouse trap than his neighbors (only Pendergast dealt not in mouse traps, but in ready mixed concrete, designed especially for county and city edifices and streets). Each who came, it is said, awaited, hat in hand, his turn, humbly presented his petition, listened to the mandate of Caesar, and backed away from the Presence.[5]

Missouri Supreme Court Commissioner John Fitzsimmons

3. Miller, *Barclay*, 51.
4. Judge Paul Barrett to author, June 23, 1987.
5. U.S. v. Pendergast, 28 F.Supp. 601, 602 (W.D. Mo. 1939).

sought election as a judge of that court, and his son met with Boss Tom's chief of staff, James Aylward. There were no letters or other correspondence, and the machine response was prompt and candid: "Can't help you now; come back in two years" was Aylward's abrupt reply to young Fitzsimmons's 1932 request.[6] Despite the oral nature of the Pendergast commitment, his word was his bond and, once given, it was never broken.

Despite his plebeian roots Pendergast combined an acute intelligence, a shrewd judgment of men, and an encyclopedic knowledge of the state of which he was the de facto ruler. Indeed, it was not happenstance that in the heyday of Pendergast's power the state capitol was known as "Uncle Tom's Cabin."

Obviously he had gone along with Governor Stark's initial appointment of Douglas, but as Douglas himself sensed in the insurance controversy another term was another matter. Pendergast's acuity had been shown by his selection of an obscure Platte County judge as the substitute Democratic candidate in 1932 when the regular nominee was killed in an automobile accident; the selectee, Judge Guy B. Park, went on to become one of the outstanding Missouri governors. Park stumbled, however, when he appointed Robert Emmet O'Malley, a Kansas City cigar stand operator and Pendergast henchman, as the state's insurance superintendent in a choice which was to have profound consequences.

O'Malley kept his job when the governorship changed hands in 1936. With Pendergast's powerful help, Lloyd Crow Stark, patrician apple grower from Louisiana, Missouri, was elected, and the machine pulled all stops in its flawed election apparatus to do so. In spite of the heady Democratic electoral victory of 1936, the rapport between the plebeian Kansas City boss and the wealthy, handsome governor was much too good to last. The first strain came with Stark's appointment of a Jackson County election board whose tendencies Pendergast perceived as a threat to the sixty thousand questionable vote registrations that were the cornerstone of his statewide power. Thereafter, the accord rapidly unraveled to the point where, reportedly, Stark never entered Jackson County without three troopers in the gubernatorial limousine—

6. Author interview with Paul Fitzsimmons, October 18, 1987.

one driving and two in back (to shield him from bullets that never came).

As Pendergast sought any stick with which to beat his enemy, a weapon presented itself by what should have been Douglas's routine re-election candidacy in 1938. Doubtless there was another factor soon to emerge: the "compromise" of the insurance rate litigation. The concordance represented not consensus but corruption wherein the real participant was the state insurance commissioner, O'Malley, fronting for his boss, Pendergast.

Douglas's breaking of the deadlock on the rate controversy probably moved Pendergast to action. The boss grasped the opportunity presented by the rival supreme court candidacy of Circuit Judge James Billings of Kennett. The *St. Louis Post-Dispatch* duly asserted that "in ordinary circumstances"[7] Douglas would be unopposed, but Billings's candidacy violated the unbroken custom in both major parties in Missouri for more than twenty-five years that an appointed judge was nominated in the next election without opposition. An acerbic critic duly noted that the *Post's* ideological propensities left the paper a less-than-reliable recorder of the traditions of the Missouri Democratic party. But there was more to the matter than this. A historian would have an easier time reviewing the confidential records of the Russian Politburo than fragmentary scraps of Thomas J. Pendergast, who committed all crucial data to memory. Records aside, there is reason to believe that this was one case in which the Kansas City pilgrimage was omitted, and the Billings candidacy launched on Pendergast's (or an associate's) initiative, possibly with peer pressure from J. V. Conran, the ruling stalwart of southeast Missouri, who may have been especially sensitive to the fact that his culturally distinct and virtually autonomous satrapy was without a representative on the state's high court.[8]

For once, the judicial election held the center of the stage. The two big-city machines split, as Mayor Bernard Dickmann's St. Louis organization closed ranks around its native son, even though it was an open question as to whether the chairmen of the Demo-

7. "What Pendergastism Means," *St. Louis Post-Dispatch*, July 31, 1938.
8. Technically, Judge C. A. Leedy's Scott County birth might have so qualified him. However, Leedy's longtime public and professional service in Jackson County made him a fully acculturated Kansas Citian.

cratic committee, Robert Hannegan and Judge Douglas, could have carried on a ten-minute social conversation.

In late July Governor Stark invaded southeast Missouri to make a rousing pro-Douglas speech in Sikeston. ("Stark Attack Carried to Billings' Ground.")[9] The event was followed by a favorable Douglas vote by the state bar convention. A flanking attack on Pendergast power came shortly thereafter when federal district Judges Reeves and Otis, the former a onetime commissioner on the state supreme court, opened a grand jury inquiry on Kansas City vote frauds. Not all the corruption was there; the St. Louis election board was unable to find 34,482 registered voters and struck their names from the rolls. Earlier the newspapers reported with a straight face the election board's explanation that no evidence of padding had been found, but incumbent Governor Park summarily turned the board out of office.

Stark carried the war to Kansas City, as charges of WPA corruption and tampering flew thick and fast. Secretary of State Dwight Brown praised Pendergast's "splendid virtues in a praying man,"[10] an encomium which proved unavailing as Douglas won the primary leading the ticket with a three-hundred-thousand majority. One issue undecided was the dilemma that the election had uncovered but not resolved—a better way to choose the members of the state's high court.[11]

9. "Stark Attack Carried to Billings' Ground," *St. Louis Post-Dispatch,* July 22, 1938.

10. "Secretary of State Backs Pendergast," *St. Louis Post-Dispatch,* July 27, 1938.

11. Southeast Missouri political folklore asserts that had the election been held a month later Billings might well have won. An intensely gregarious and outgoing person as well as a vigorous campaigner, he customarily shook the hand of every person present (including criminal defendants awaiting sentence) before opening court. While in a filling station during his twenty-five thousand miles of driving in 1938, he introduced himself and shook the hand of a lady who responded, "Why, I'm your wife."

22

The Missouri Plan

The bitter primary of 1938 spilled over into the general election two years later. By singular coincidence, the exacerbated Billings-Douglas battle and the unprecedented effort of the political boss to work his will on a high court climaxed a movement that had been stirring underground for decades. That was the search for a satisfactory solution to the question of whether judges should be appointed or elected. Missouri had struggled with the problem from almost the moment of its admission to the Union. The original constitution of 1820 adopted the federal appointive model—the governor named the judges of the supreme and circuit courts with the advice and consent of the state senate. Once in place, the judges served until age sixty with assurance against salary cuts.

The veto by the state judiciary of the relief legislation of 1821 stirred up resentment against the court as a politically irresponsible arm of government (see chap. 3). These sentiments came as part of a general wave of democratic liberalization, including, in particular, the extension of voting privileges and abolition of property qualifications. By 1846, Missouri joined the general consensus of the states by limiting judicial terms to twelve years. The Jacksonian elective principle completely triumphed by 1849 when a constitutional amendment established short terms and frequent accountability. The amendment further reduced the supreme court judges' term to six years. The governor lost the power of appointment; the amendment provided for the election of judges in the general elections. However, an effort at greater insulation of the judicial selection process from politics appeared in a provision of the amendment scheduling judicial elections in the summer following the elections for the legislative and executive branches.

The situation remained essentially unchanged by the constitutions of 1865 and 1875. The problem also remained unchanged. The dilemma was that within the democratic process, judges had to be exempt from that process. This was true, notwithstanding the separation of powers as extolled by Montesquieu, Blackstone, and the constitutional framers. The dilemma was neatly summarized by a delegate to the abortive constitutional convention of 1845:

> A judicial officer is different from a mere political officer, a judge is the organ of the law, a political officer of the people. . . . [As] Chief Justice Marshall [said] A judge has no will of his own; he is a mere instrument of the law; he is bound, governed and guided by the law; it is his polestar which alone guides his decisions. How then could a judge . . . that power which stands between the people and the government, but subject to the sway of the people, and be bound by their instructions?[1]

The fundamental flaw in pure democratic choice was underscored by a variety of proposals, all recoiling from the unqualified elective principle, and all proposing some variant of executive appointment. The core of the difficulty lay in the consensus that while selection methods might be modified, the body politic of necessity had to retain the power of dismissal.

Indeed, by the 1920s the complications of traditional democratic selection had led theorists as diverse as American conservative William Howard Taft and British socialist Harold Laski to score the existing system in favor of innovative reform. Taft had earlier faulted political selection. Laski suggested separation of the nomination and appointment processes.[2] The Laski "separation," which left appointment to a politically responsible governor, who could choose from a list of prescreened eligible nominees drawn by a nonpartisan commission, lost at the polls in referenda

1. William C. Jones of Newton County quoted in Jack Pettison, "The Missouri Plan for the Selection of Judges," 23–24.

2. Harold J. Laski, "The Technique of Judicial Appointment," 24 Mich. L. Rev. 529 (1926).

in both Michigan and Ohio. Such gallant but unsuccessful efforts to legislate separation provided valuable lessons for reformers elsewhere. But even reform had its own problems. A California experiment retained gubernatorial appointment but subjected it to confirmation by a Committee on Qualifications. The experiment floundered. The committee quickly became a rubber stamp of powerful executives, and the old flaws of the appointive system were resurrected in new garb.

The reform movement had its own Missouri manifestation. In 1934 the supreme court under its rule-making power established the Judicial Council.[3] The council provided an institutionalized framework that afforded focus and direction to the otherwise diffused forces of discontent with the status quo. The council consisted of eleven members—nine appointed by the court and the chairmen of the judiciary committees of the General Assembly. Political developments within the state provided the major impetus to reform in Missouri.

Especially noteworthy during this time was the rise of the classic big city machines in St. Louis and Kansas City. St. Louis was a case in point, even when dominated by an inept albeit amiable Republican organization. Their effort seldom included elevation of outright incompetents to the bench. As a result, the endorsements of the St. Louis Bar Association, plus editorial pronouncements by the *St. Louis Post-Dispatch*, assured the continuity of high-caliber courts during the 1920s.

All this changed with the advent of the Great Depression and the rise of the so-called Dickmann-Hannegan Democratic machine. To the machine, a circuit judgeship differed little from an appointment in the Water Department. Final selection occurred in a summer primary, for which endorsement on the machine's sample ballot equated to nomination and subsequent election. Customarily, the ballot carried the names of the judicial candidates at the end of its long list of contested offices. Here, place alone guaranteed voter disinterest by the general populace. The compact and resolute cadre of machine adherents and precinct followers elected the judges, either by doggedly voting a straight ticket or by following their sample ballot to its very end.

3. Supreme Court Rule 39, 334 Mo. xix–xx.

As a result, Democratic victories, beginning with the municipal elections of 1933, swept the St. Louis bench clean of Republicans. A year later, a neighborhood druggist with a law degree won both the primary and the general election for a six-year term in spite of not winning the St. Louis Bar's endorsement. Local papers later described his performance as a humiliation to the law and the city. Among his failures were the almost total incompetence of a "stacked" grand jury to investigate election frauds and a scandalous receivership of a warehouse company. Forty years later, senior St. Louis attorney Harold Hancke recalled trying a case before the druggist-judge in which opposing counsel was Robert Hannegan, chairman of the Democratic City Committee. Hancke remembered that the court glanced at Hannegan for the latter's covert approval or disapproval before ruling on Hancke's objections.[4]

Against this background, the forces of change converged in 1936 when the Missouri Judicial Council proposed to amend the state constitution to provide for the nomination of judicial candidates at party conventions called solely for that purpose. There was a singular irony here. The primary had been instituted with the high hope of ending the evils of convention selection, but that high hope ended with the unforeseen rise of machine politics of a character and magnitude undreamed of by Boss Butler and the "Boodlers."

Kenneth Teasdale, a St. Louis lawyer and the president of the Missouri Bar, supplied a key alteration with a proposal to adopt Laski's suggestion—nominations by a small group and actual appointment by the governor—in lieu of convention selection.[5] A second and most practical idea came from a theoretical source, academician Charles T. McCormick who proposed preserving ultimate democratic choice by subjecting judges to postappointment retention or ouster by popular vote. Under Teasdale's leadership the kaleidoscopic forces of change coalesced into a Missouri Institute for the Administration of Justice, founded in Columbia in the closing days of 1937. The institute's activities were fuelled by an anonymous donation from St. Louis civic leader Luther Ely

4. Author interview with Harold Hancke, June 21, 1990.
5. Kenneth Teasdale, The President's Letter, 8 J. Mo. B. 34 (1937).

Smith, Jr., and sparked by the genius of a Manhattan public relations man, M. B. Marshall.

After initial failures, which included attempts to confer substantive rule-making power on the judiciary and to launch a referendum from the legislature, the institute undertook the herculean task of obtaining the requisite number of signatures in the required number of congressional districts to put the nonpartisan court plan on the ballot for a referendum at the November 1940 election.

The institute was headquartered in St. Louis's Boatmen's Bank building and had regional offices throughout the state. The headlines of its *News* told the story of its efforts to obtain the needed signatures: "Petitions for Non-Partisan Court Plan Being Circulated in All Congressional Districts" (April 15, 1940) and "Campaign Chairmen Now Appointed in 57 Counties" (May 15, 1940). The planners hoped to obtain seventy-five thousand signatures, which was more than needed to place the nonpartisan court plan on the ballot. They succeeded. The institute beat the professional politicians at their own game by mounting a grass-roots statewide political effort. As a headline of the institute's *News* proclaimed: "Place on Ballot Assured" (July 15, 1940).

As the general election of 1940 approached, the efforts of the institute rose to a crescendo. The campaign was staged against the background of a bitter Democratic primary during the summer. The residue of the confrontation carried on into the fall. This in turn guaranteed a substantial turnout of citizens disposed to support reform but not inclined to make a major effort for it. As another fortuitous development, Boss Pendergast's preoccupation with the gubernatorial campaign diverted him from overt and extended opposition to court reform.

The tactical commander of the electorial effort was Professor Israel Treiman of the Washington University School of Law. He brilliantly integrated the specific features of the grand design: (1) the Laski thesis of separating the nomination and appointive process and (2) the McCormick additive, which preserved a democratic safety catch by providing for postappointive approval (or rejection) by elections in which the incumbent judge ran unopposed. In its origins, the nonpartisan court plan was mandatory for the circuit and probate courts of St. Louis City and Jackson County, and the state supreme court and the three regional courts of appeal. It was left optional for the circuit and probate courts of the other circuits of the state. Two commissions controlled the nominating process: an appellate nominating commission of seven (three laymen and three lawyers, chaired by the presiding judge of the regional court of appeals) and a circuit panel similarly structured.

Thanks to the mobilization of strategically placed interest groups—the metropolitan newspapers (especially the *St. Louis Post-Dispatch*, with its drumbeat of anti-Pendergast cartoons), the organized bar generally, and the League of Women Voters—the plan rolled to a smashing victory in November; it received 535,642 votes out of close to a million cast, or 45,224 more than enough to provide the necessary amendment of the state constitution.

There were some sidelights. The low estate of the St. Louis courts helped the victory. In litigating the deductibility of lawyer contributions to the Missouri Institute for the Administration of Justice in a test case carried by Luther Ely Smith, Jr., the Board of Tax Appeals reportedly ruled: (1) the institute was *not* an "educational, religious, or philanthropic organization" for which deductibility was allowed for philanthropic reasons, *but* (2) the mediocrity of the local courts permitted contributions as a business expense by lawyer-donors. A significant insight into the state of the local courts had emerged at a meeting of the St. Louis Bar a few years earlier. When Mark D. Eagleton took the floor to praise some local judges as above average, his reference reportedly evoked a burst of laughter from his audience.

The nonpartisan court plan had its real acid test a few years later when some hardened, last-ditch partisans, cynically manipulating the argument that the plan was "undemocratic," sought its repeal by a statewide referendum. Even though they were operating without the enthusiasm and euphoria of the initial effort to establish the plan, the proponents held fast. They secured a majority at the polls to ensure that the plan had at least some breathing time and a chance for long-term survival in the future.

23

Fall of a Titan

His name was Thomas Pendergast, and the state supreme court made him. It could also be fairly said that the court ultimately broke him. His rule over Jackson County and Kansas City began in 1932 when that court refused to command the municipal legislature to fund the budget of the independently appointed police board.[1]

The police function had always been a problem in Missouri. During the Civil War, one of the major acts of the 1861 constitutional convention had been to remove it from the governmental powers of secession-sympathizing St. Louis. Indeed, even under the "liberation" constitution of 1875 (which granted home rule to St. Louis), the police were administered by the state rather than the city. The reasons were obvious: the paramilitary police were a handy instrument of coercion. (The supreme court ouster of 1865 was accomplished by policemen, not soldiers.) Moreover, under Boss Butler's hegemony in St. Louis, the required presence of a patrolman in each polling place actually became a mechanism of electoral fraud; citizens who protested manifest irregularity too loudly were apt to find themselves taken to the nearest station and charged with peace disturbance.

Control of police hiring and promotion served as the wedge by which the Pendergasts (first his brother then the boss himself)

1. State *ex rel.* Field v. Smith, 49 S.W.2d 74 (Mo. en banc 1932).

gradually took over the entire governmental apparatus of Kansas City, including the electoral machinery where tens of thousands of questionable registrations provided a solid base of support not only in the city itself, but throughout the state. Innocent enough at first, the mere existence of such power corrupted, and the town became something of a sinkhole of iniquity. As veteran attorney Robert Hyder described it, "Kansas City was wide open":

> I found 429 slot machines within a block of the courthouse, and it was a felony to have one in your place of business. . . . In four years the prosecuting attorney had not filed a single car theft case, and if you parked your car and didn't have a certain little red tag on the steering wheel of your car they'd have it dismantled in five minutes. I mean it was horrible. . . . And, oh, it was unbelievable the things they did at some of these night spots.[2]

Paul Fitzsimmons, son of a state supreme court judge and one-time law dean, corroborated Hyder's view of Kansas City in the mid 1930s: "I saw things there I never saw in Paris."[3]

By the late 1930s Pendergast's iron grip was beginning to slip. Attorney General McKittrick's ouster suits lanced the most blatant sores by turning the sheriff and the prosecuting attorney out of office. Concurrently, federal district Judges Reeves and Otis strongly backed the efforts of U.S. attorney, Maurice Milligan (appointed from Washington and hence insulated from Pendergast power), to launch an investigation of widespread election fraud.

In the boss's case, external attack combined with interior neurosis. Pendergast's otherwise acute intelligence and puritanical Irish morality were flawed at one critical point to almost a psychotic degree: "His hobbies are horse-racing and blooded horses," goes a contemporary report. "Annually he makes trips to Saratoga Springs, New York, and other eastern racing courses. . . . The Louisville Derby always finds him an interested spectator."[4] Hand in hand with a love of horseflesh went a love of betting. ("He was crazy about money for horse races.")[5] The need for gambling funds

2. Depositional interview of Robert Hyder, Supreme Court Historical Society, Jefferson City, Missouri.
3. Author interview with Paul Fitzsimmons, October 18, 1987.
4. William Rufus Jackson, *Missouri Democracy: A History of the Party and Its Representative Members—Past and Present,* 647.
5. Hyder interview, n. 2.

and the insurance rate litigation converged to form a deadly combination. The hat was later passed in undocumented meetings with the insurers whose contributions were keyed to anticipated benefits. Successive cash payments were delivered by an air-borne courier. Altogether $315,000 was delivered, Pendergast allegedly "laying over" (to use racetrack parlance) $22,500 to Insurance Superintendent O'Malley. Reportedly, Pendergast gambled away the payoff within one week on racetrack bets. The insurers had gotten quite a bargain from the insurance superintendent: 80 percent of the (past) impounded premiums and 90 percent of the (future) self-help 16 $2/3$ percent rate increase. The District Court of Western Missouri duly approved the "compromise" and it seemed the rate controversy was at last at an end.

But not quite. Prosecutor Milligan and the *Post-Dispatch* filled in details: In 1935 Insurance Superintendent O'Malley came to St. Louis and asked one A. L. McCormack, a lobbyist-operator insurance executive, if the insurance companies might wish to settle the seemingly interminable rate litigation. McCormack crawfished, asserting his lack of authority but offering to transmit any concrete offer to C. R. Street in Chicago, a vice-president of six insurance companies. O'Malley then cast the bait: "Maybe if Mr. Street would talk with Mr. Pendergast . . . they might be able to get together and dispose of the case."[6] A Chicago meeting was arranged between Street and Pendergast and a settlement fee of $500,000 (subject to being raised to $750,000 for expedition) was arranged.

Pendergast took the insurers' money courteously enough and remembered to say "Thank you" when the cash changed hands.[7] But what he forgot to do was to share the spoils with his own government and avoid the fate of Al Capone. The latter had been imprisoned in 1931 for failing to pay income tax on his ill-gotten gains. When indicted, Pendergast duly pleaded guilty to evading taxes on his enhanced $750,000 payoff; as to the pittance of $22,500 which went to O'Malley, the latter also pleaded guilty and was likewise sent to prison. (Both were also cited for contempt.) State pros-

6. American Ins. Co. v. Lucas, 38 F. Supp. 896, 907 (W.D. Mo. 1940).
7. State *ex inf.* Taylor v. American Ins. Co., 200 S.W.2d 1, 28 (Mo. en banc 1946).

ecution was something else again, and current controversy was darkened by the long shadow of *Butler*, which determined that a bribe taker must have a statutory authority to deliver the goods (see chap. 15). Governor Stark anxiously wrote Attorney General McKittrick to "find out if there is any state law to convict a public official who has accepted a bribe for taking [$]3,000,000 from 800,000 Mo. policyholders."[8] McKittrick replied that he did not know whether any state law had been violated.

However, the reverberations of the bribe did not end with the jailing of the boss, and the impact of the state supreme court on rate litigation continued. One of its former members, Ray Lucas, was appointed insurance commissioner when Governor Stark dismissed O'Malley. Lucas, who bore the title judge with dignity, had been one of the shortest serving judges, having sat for three and a half months in 1938. He got specific marching orders from the governor as to the court-approved compromise: "I, therefore, charge you as Commissioner of Insurance for the State of Missouri to join in a written request to the Court that a full and complete report be required."[9] He did so, and the federal district court summarized the problem in words that suggested its obvious solution: "The settlement was procured by bribery and . . . fraud was committed upon this court when it was induced to make that agreement effective."[10] The court accordingly voided the "compromise" and decreed a full return to the policyholders.

Even though the letter of the law provided punishment only to the bribee, the law of the ancient writ of quo warranto had been shaped by the Missouri Supreme Court to provide sanctions as well as ouster for illegal or unwarranted corporate activity (see chap. 25). The court duly applied the doctrine when fines of at least $10,000 were levied against each of the 122 miscreant insurers on the second-to-last day of 1946.[11]

The action came twenty-four years after Insurance Superintendent Hyde had issued his rate reduction order. It was some-

8. "Insurance Department," Lloyd C. Stark Papers, Western Manuscripts Historical Collection, State Historical Society of Missouri, Columbia, Missouri.

9. Stark to Lucas, Memorandum, February 8, 1939, Stark Papers, n. 8.

10. *American Ins. Co.* 38 F. Supp. at 922.

11. *American Ins. Co.*, 200 S.W.2d at 53–55.

thing of a triumph for the commissioner system; commissioners Henry I. Westhues and S. P. Dalton undertook a herculean labor in framing a decree conformable to the monstrous thirty-two-thousand-page record. The decree should have been the dramatic last act in the controversy. It was not. A more dramatic, if dissonant, climax of the rate litigation was suggested by a terse notation at the end of the decree: "All the Judges concur, except Gantt, J., not sitting."[12]

12. *Id.* at 55.

24

The Great Feud

The most dramatic of the consequences of the insurance rate litigation actually came second to last. It was recorded by a three-column headline in the *St. Louis Post-Dispatch* on May 5, 1942: "Feud in Supreme Court, Gantt's Opinions Barred; He Quits As Chief Justice." The feud resulted from Superintendent Lucas's efforts to do justice for the policyholders, and in this respect he proved as aggressive as his predecessor had been flaccid. One avenue of recovery was the attempted recapture of some $289,000 of impounded premiums that had been paid out by the Central Missouri Trust Company under order of the Circuit Court of Cole County. The payouts were for salary to the "custodians" of the fund, Cook and Lauf, as well as for legal fees, stenographic and clerical help, stationery and supplies, office rent, and the like. The payments were called into question by the state supreme court's blockbuster ruling that the insurance commissioner was the sole legal custodian of the impounded rate increases. Commissioner Lucas pounced on the ruling. He insisted that the circuit court's absence of jurisdiction made the payout orders null and void and entailed liability to the depositary bank for the disbursements. However, in fairness it must be pointed out that FDIC insurance covered only a fraction of the deposit, and memories of bank failure during the depression prompted unceasing surveillance of depositaries.

Was the bank liable? There was no clear answer under the obscure statute that had caused all the trouble in the first place. Nonetheless, it seemed utterly unjust to impose such liability retroactively and require the bank to have clairvoyant foresight in dealing with funds under court order. On the other hand, the Central Missouri Trust was the centerpiece of what was colloquially known as the "establishment," and the bank *must* have been cynically knowledgeable that the custodian arrangement was a typical exercise whereby political boodle was distributed to the politically favored for little or no work.[1]

Lucas's quest for a refund had come on his appeal from an adverse judgment in the Circuit Court of Jackson County. Under the supreme court's administrative procedure, the appeal was first argued in division one where two opinions, neither of which received majority support, were proposed. The inconclusive result caused the case to be transferred before all seven judges, en banc.

Before the entire court, the case produced four published opinions.[2] The majority view, written by Judge Albert A. Clark, rejected Lucas's contention that the bank should have known that its handling of the fund was without formal sanction. Judge George Robb Ellison concurred, observing that Lucas's argument of "constructive knowledge of the law" would require a court appointee to be "wiser than the court he serves." He denounced the idea as obviously and viciously unsound and productive of confusion and peril.[3] Judges Leedy and Tipton concurred in the Clark opinion, and Judge Douglas also concurred in a separate opinion. Judge Charles Hays dissented holding that the bank had clearly been forewarned of this peril by the court's previous judgment; he also limited interest on the improvident payments to those accruing after October 17, 1938, the date when the character of the impounded fund was unequivocally clarified. Chief Justice Ernest Gantt unlimbered a devastating dissent holding that on the law and the evidence the bank was clearly liable. But he went further yet, suggesting that political considerations

1. Richard A. Watson and Rondal Downing, *The Politics of the Bench and Bar: Judging Selection under the Missouri Nonpartisan Court Plan*, 166–67, 170–73.
2. Lucas v. Central Missouri Trust Co., 162 S.W. 2d 569 (Mo. en banc 1942).
3. "Feud in Supreme Court," *St. Louis Post-Dispatch*, May 5, 1942.

underlay the majority opinion, and that the court itself was under the domination of the Pendergast machine. Judge Tipton wrote a "replv opinion," not addressed to the legal issue under consideration but to his colleague, the chief justice, whom he accused of accepting Pendergast support.

There was no question that Gantt was outraged by the record before him. The last of the tobacco-chewing judges (he often borrowed a "chaw" of Tinsley's Fine-Cut from nearby lawyers), he was a man of old-fashioned virtue and intense tranquility. He wore string ties (especially ordered in St. Louis) and frequently took his lunch to court in a brown paper bag along with a bottle of buttermilk, carrying both bag and bottle home at day's end to be recycled. During the hot Jefferson City summers he usually went to and from court in shirtsleeves, a practice which caused him on one occasion to be identified as the day janitor of the building.[4]

Gantt's dissent must have been mildness itself alongside the verbal exchanges that took place when the refund issue was discussed in conference. No question that Gantt's rage was fuelled not only by the sleazy, cynical arrangement itself but by his colleagues' attitude in tolerating it. The latter perception boiled over into scathing comments.

Colleagues, essentially innocent bystanders, drew their own blasts. Judge James Douglas was assailed as simplistic and lachrymose: "In writing the opinion he used the 'simple language' method. The 'simple language' method as illustrated by his opinion means to ignore all the material facts and rule the case on mere conclusions. . . . He writes feelingly about the trust company receiving the money. In writing his opinion he from time to time must have paused to weep." The gentle and gentlemanly George Robb Ellison found himself moved to verbosity: "Ellison, J. writes and he writes and he writes. He also repeats and repeats and repeats."[5]

Several targets of Gantt's wrath were moved to submit reply

4. *Mexico Evening Ledger*, March 5, 1947. See also *State Bar Pays Tribute to Supreme Court*, J. Mo. B. March 1930 at 2.
5. The actual dissent appears to have been lost. In those prephotocopying days, carbon copies (six at most) were made. An expurgated version of the dissent was carried in the *St. Louis Post-Dispatch*, May 29, 1942, "Gantt Says People Should Blow Court Out of Existence."

opinions. All, save one, were withdrawn. Tipton chose to stand his ground on the issue of Pendergast support. But Gantt chose to stand *his* ground too: Tipton "states that Pendergast supported me in the primary election of 1936. They think because of that support I should join them in [the majority] opinion. I am not of that variety."[6]

Judge Gantt was not finished. After perusing what his colleagues had to say about his views in "reply" opinions of judges Tipton, Clark, Ellison, and Leedy (the latter three subsequently withdrawn) he cut loose with a reply of his own. Its thrust was captured in a headline: "Gantt in Reply Declares That 'People Should Blow Court Out of Existence.' "[7]

His brethren, however, had the last word. In an unprecedented 4–2 vote the court refused to permit the filing of three opinions, two by Gantt and one by Tipton. The court's action was based on a finding that the material therein was scandalous, impertinent, and scurrilous. An especially bitter note was provided by the action of the court's clerk, Eppa Elliott, who came from Gantt's hometown of Mexico, Missouri, and who in a measure owed his job to Judge Gantt, in refusing to receive the judge's tender of his unwelcome views when presented for the official record.

Gantt immediately resigned as chief justice of the court and as presiding judge of division one. Judge Ellison was elected to take his place. The bitter feeling was not at an end with Judge Gantt going on something of a strike by refusing to sit in on further conferences or to participate in subsequent proceedings on the rate controversy. He therefore did not vote on the ultimate issue which his rebellion provoked: a motion that the supreme court rehear the case on the grounds that suppression of the dissents violated basic procedural norms. The court stood fast on its suppression but did make one concession: if the case went to the U.S. Supreme

6. *St. Louis Post-Dispatch*, May 29, 1942. Possibly Judge Tipton's snappishness resulted from family problems. His sister, Nellie Tipton Muench, had become involved in a Gothic sequence of kidnapping, seduction, extortion, and mail fraud. During her trial in Mexico, Missouri, the judge sat faithfully by her side. See Ernest Kirschten, *Catfish and Crystal*, 300–301; State v. Rosegrant, 93 S.W. 2d 961 (Mo. Div. 2 1936); and Muench v. United States, 96 Fed. 332 (8th Cir. 1938).

7. "Blow Court Out of Existence," *St. Louis Post-Dispatch*, May 29, 1942.

"Smoke from Our Rumbling Volcano." *St. Louis Post-Dispatch*, photograph courtesy of State Historical Society of Missouri, Columbia.

Court, the excluded opinions could accompany the record to the high tribunal under seal.

The concession scarcely mollified the storm of protest the ruling created. Predictably, the metropolitan press fulminated. The *St. Louis Post-Dispatch* solemnly intoned, "Judge Gantt Does Not Stand Alone," and condemned the court's judgment on both substance and procedure.[8] The blast was accompanied by a Fitzpatrick cartoon where escaping smoke from a smothered volcano entitled "Judge Gantt's Suppressed Opinion" spelled out: "$289,000 Whose Money Is It?" And from far away Cambridge, the *Harvard Law Review* added its criticism under the case note "Courts— Majority of Court Prevents Filing of Opinion of Dissenting Chief Justice."[9]

Bluster to the contrary, Attorney General McKittrick did not take the case to the U.S. Supreme Court. Despite sonorous headlines ("Suppression of Gantt Dissent Expected to Figure in Missouri Political Campaigns This Year"), the cause célèbre petered out and died.[10] So did Judge Gantt sometime later and possibly of a broken heart. He seldom sat en banc after *Lucas;* he retired December 31, 1946, and died of a heart attack the following March. Lieutenant Governor Harris gave the eulogy at the "strictly private" (a coded injunction to his former colleagues to stay away) funeral held at the Arnold Funeral Home in Mexico. Not a single member of his court was present.

---

8. *Id.*

9. See *Courts—Majority of Court Prevents Filing of Opinion of Dissenting Chief Justice,* 56 Har. L. Rev. 472 (1942).

10. "Blow Court Out of Existence," *St. Louis Post-Dispatch,* May 29, 1942.

LIGHTS AND SHADOWS

25

Foiling the Great Governorship "Steal"

On March 14, 1940, Lawrence "Larry" McDaniel filed for the Democratic nomination for governor of Missouri. McDaniel was a longtime party warhorse and St. Louis's excise (liquor) commissioner. Traditionally Democratic, Missouri had customarily taken its governors from that party, and the strong possibility of FDR's presence on the ticket for an unprecedented third term made McDaniel's prospects bright indeed.

There were drawbacks. Able, good-looking Allen McReynolds of Carthage was in the field as a party rival. Worse yet, the seeming Democratic hegemony masked an uneasy alliance between the big city machines in Bernard Dickmann's St. Louis and Thomas Pendergast's Kansas City. With the courthouse "rings" in Protestant outstate Missouri, Pendergast in particular had come under attack in 1932 when urbane patrician Russell Dearmont sought the governorship and strongly attacked the Kansas City machine's influence in state affairs. The reformist assault was renewed in the bitter supreme court primary election of 1938 between James Billings and James Douglas.

McDaniel had other disadvantages. Despite being a Methodist Sunday school teacher, his portly, owl-eyed appearance was reminiscent of an archetypical Irish Catholic politician, particularly Boss Tom Pendergast. He was pilloried mercilessly by the cartoonists, but the machine's power held and he rolled to victory in the primary. His style carried over to the general election where he used two lines with great effect to rouse the Democratic faithful. He customarily opened his speeches, "The question is not when do we eat? but *do* we eat?" He closed them with the peroration that endorsed the third term of FDR and attacked the public utility past of Wendell Willkie, the GOP nominee: "Let's keep Willkie in the powerhouse and Roosevelt in the White House!" Sitting as a copartisan Democratic candidate on the same platform at the political rallies with McDaniel around the state, Supreme Court Judge George Robb Ellison ("a gentleman among gentlemen" according to colleague Paul Barrett) listened airily—possibly hoping, thanks to the nonpartisan court proposal on the same ballot, that he might be hearing such hokum for the last time.[1]

It was the bitterest primary in memory, and the residue carried into November where the entire Democratic ticket swept to victory with one exception: Republican Forrest Donnell of Webster Groves won the governorship by a margin of 3,616 votes out of close to a million cast. The result was truly a Democratic disaster, for the governorship with a cornucopia of appointments of judgeships, boards, commissions, and like offices was the jewel in the patronage crown. Worse yet, the transfer of the office to the GOP might well spark a renaissance of the seemingly moribund minority. "The Democrats could not reconcile themselves to the fact that they had lost the governorship," recalled veteran St. Louis lawyer Richmond Coburn.[2] Within hours of the election C. Marion Hulen of Mexico, chairman of the state Democratic Committee, was darkly hinting of pervasive vote fraud and massive vote-buying.[3] On November 13, 1940, five major Democrats—U.S. Senator Bennett Champ Clark, St. Louis Mayor Bernard F. Dickmann, St. Louis Democratic party chairman Robert Hannegan, Attorney General Roy McKittrick, and state Democratic chairman C. Marion Hulen, along with several identified smaller fry (Charles M. Hay, St. Louis election board chairman, State Senator Michael Kinney, Secretary of State Dwight Brown, and An-

1. Letter from Judge Barrett to the author, June 23, 1987.
2. Depositional interview of Richmond Coburn, December 27, 1985, Supreme Court of Missouri Historical Society, Jefferson City, Missouri.
3. See David D. March, *The History of Missouri* (New York: Lewis Historical Pub. Co., 1967), 1421.

thony A. Buford, Anheuser-Busch legislative counsel)—gathered at St. Louis's DeSoto Hotel (regular rate $3 per night) instead of the Democrats' regular gathering place, the old Jefferson Hotel, for a postmortem. They met amid sporadic reports of Republican electoral wrongdoing. As Coburn recalled, "They got together and decided to handle the matter by means of a provision in the Constitution of Missouri [which provides] that in case of an election for governor . . . the speaker of the House of Representatives in the presence of the members of the House and Senate would count—tabulate—the votes and then proclaim to the general public who had won."[4]

The meeting strikingly exemplified the jape of comedian Will Rogers that he belonged to no organized political party but instead was a Democrat. The affair was totally unstructured. It had neither rules of order, agenda, nor presiding officer; participants floated in and out of the room all afternoon, coming and going at will as knots of conversationalists severally discussed the electoral disaster and its consequence for their own prospects.

Typical was the experience of Buford, the Anheuser-Busch attorney, who had encountered Hannegan in a chance meeting on Locust Street. When Hannegan disclosed that he was en route to the DeSoto to meet Senator Clark, Buford went along in the hope of discussing pending federal legislation. The opportunity never really materialized, and instead Buford subsequently found his picture on the front page of the *Post-Dispatch*, which implied he was a putative conspirator in a latter-day Gunpowder Plot.[5]

Senator Clark later described the gathering as a "gabfest" and Hannegan issued a written statement characterizing it as a quasi-social forgathering of copartisans, devoid of any sinister purpose.[6] Possibly (as Coburn noted) there was discussion of Article V of the Missouri Constitution, which provided in an obvious analog to the U.S. Constitution for delivery of certified election returns to the Speaker of the House for tabulation and announcement at a joint session of the state legislature. Discussion, such as it was,

4. Coburn deposition, n. 4.
5. "Inside Story of How Donnell-McDaniel 'Contest' Began," *St. Louis Post-Dispatch*, January 30, 1941.
6. "Hannegan Says Hotel Meeting Wasn't Secret," *St. Louis Post-Dispatch*, January 30, 1941.

could well have focused on exploiting this provision under some plausible factual base. The meeting of the DeSoto group broke up, apparently leaving it to State Chairman Hulen to decide whether the reports of Republican fraud were substantial enough to require offsetting legislative action. The Republicans had always constantly beaten the Democrats in fund-raising, which the latter suspected that the bulging GOP war chest had spilled over into vote-buying and other irregularity.

Hulen (probably the real architect of the maneuver) perfected it at a meeting of the Democratic State Committee in Jefferson City on December 30, 1940, and structured it on the role of the Speaker of the House. Coburn's indecision on the difference between "count" and "tabulate" marked the jewelled pivot-point of the DeSoto plot, which hinged on whether the Speaker (1) could only read the face of the election certificates or (2) had discretion to go behind those documents and verify their recitations. The difference was critical, for the accession of the governor depended on the Speaker's announcement. If held up long enough, sufficient fraud—3,617 flawed votes would do it—might be found in GOP strongholds to undo the overall electoral result. It was a brilliant stroke that bypassed the tedious and expensive legal recount procedure, which required that the nominal winner be seated pending any outcome and enjoy all the powers, privileges, and patronage of office in the interim. Only one sour note was sounded. Canny Attorney General McKittrick publicly warned that in addition to investigation costs of $25,000, the Machiavellian ploy could backfire in that the St. Louis machine faced a spring election, whereas the "country boys" had two years to ride out any incipient scandal.[7]

On January 8, 1941, the General Assembly convened in Jefferson City. A House caucus bound the Democratic majority to support the preemptive strike of deferred announcement that was duly enacted into Resolution No. 3 of the General Assembly forbidding the Speaker to take action until a special legislative committee had reexamined the ballots. Attorney General McKittrick told his copartisans in the state senate that the proposal to bar Donnell was perfectly legal. On January 10, the returns were de-

7. "Inside Story," *St. Louis Post-Dispatch*, January 30, 1941.

livered to House Speaker Morris Osburn, but as the Missouri Supreme Court later recited, he "declined" to announce the result to declare Donnell governor, asserting he was forbidden to do so by Joint Resolution No. 3.[8]

The ostensible legal basis of the resolution was the filing of a complaint of the Democratic State Committee charging fraud in the gubernatorial vote and asking for a legislative investigation. Many country Democratic organizations filed similar resolutions, and a singular private one came from future governor and son of a one-time member of the supreme court, James T. Blair, Jr., acting as "a citizen and voter of Cole County."[9] Accordingly, the assembly passed Joint Resolution No. 3, which was duly vetoed by Governor Stark; the veto was ignored as a joint committee moved to investigate and recount the ballots.

Under the state constitution, the new governor's term began January 13. On that day Chief Justice Leedy routinely swore in the statewide Democratic ticket minus McDaniel. The Donnell inaugural was postponed, and Lloyd Stark became the first holdover governor in Missouri history. That same day, instead of taking his inaugural oath, Donnell filed a petition in the state supreme court for the ancient common law writ of mandamus.[10]

Mandamus (we command) is a judicial order to a public officer to perform a public duty as to which the law affords the officer no choice. The tactic had been chosen by a trio of Republican lawyers, James A. Finch, Sr. (Cape Girardeau), Frank Atwood, a former member of the supreme court (Jefferson City), and Charles E. Rendlen (Hannibal).[11] It was a simple, streamlined solution: the Speaker was merely to announce—not recount—the election results.

Donnell filed a second suit in prohibition which was exactly opposite of mandamus: a judicial command to an individual, a body, or a court forbidding it to take action outside its legal jurisdiction.[12] This sought to bar the joint legislative committee (called the Searcy Committee after its chairman, Senator L. N.

8. State *ex rel.* Donnell v. Osburn, 147 S.W.2d 1065, 1067 (Mo. en banc 1941).
9. *Id.*
10. *Id.*
11. Interestingly, the sons of Rendlen and Finch later sat on the Missouri Supreme Court.
12. State *ex rel.* Donnell v. Searcy, 152 S.W.2d 8 (Mo. en banc 1941).

Searcy) from recounting the ballots, particularly in view of an existing legal procedure on the books. The two cases were argued together on February 11, 1941, Chief Justice Leedy ordering the matters consolidated for hearing and expedited in view of their obvious importance. St. Louis lawyers Richmond Coburn and Richard Shewmaker, staunch Democrats, joined the original Republican trio to argue the prohibition action and give a bipartisan color to the effort.

The questions of the judges indicated the temper of the court. Judge Gantt, the tribunal's curmudgeon, hammered Attorney General McKittrick particularly hard at the mandamus hearing the moment the latter opened his mouth and began his argument. ("Where is there anything in those plain and simple words that authorizes what you are defending?")[13] During his argument on the prohibition suit, Coburn asked the judges: "What are they trying to do? Make a governor out of Morris Osburn?" He added, "And they all laughed. We felt we were getting along pretty well with the Court when they reacted that way."[14]

The hilarity on the supreme court bench produced by the mere thought of the Speaker exercising gubernatorial authority with the proclamation power was not matched elsewhere. Instead a firestorm of protest swept the state. Coburn recalled that "the uproar . . . exceeded anything I ever saw. People just went crazy, and they were just—oh, the reaction against the Democratic leadership and functions that were being exercised was terrific. And that had a good deal to do with what happened ultimately in the litigation."[15] The cynicism of the parliamentary maneuver, based on the preposterous idea that the corrupt political machines had been beaten at their own game of stealing votes and stuffing ballot boxes was pilloried in a Daniel Fitzpatrick cartoon in the *St. Louis Post-Dispatch* ("On to Jefferson City") wherein two portly, cigar-chomping politicians representing the St. Louis and Kansas City machines under the placard "We Was Robbed" led a parade: "Ghost Voters' Club," "Vacant Lot Voters' Club," "Repeaters' Club," "Red Light Club," "Flophouse Club." Bringing up the

13. "Donnell Suit Argued," *St. Louis Post-Dispatch*, February 11, 1941.
14. Coburn depositional interview.
15. *Id.*

"On to Jefferson City!" *St. Louis Post-Dispatch*, photograph courtesy of State Historical Society of Missouri, Columbia.

rear was a tow truck carrying McDaniel astride a moribund Democratic donkey.[16] The *Post's* condemnation of the steal was matched by the censure of its local rival, the *Globe-Democrat*, and the *Kansas City Star*. In rural Missouri the reaction was the same except for a few incorrigibly partisan organs like the *Lewiston Times*. The *Post's* cartoon presented by Fitzpatrick's stiletto-pen was devastating. Indeed, thanks to corrosive ridicule, what began as a degradation of the democratic process rapidly became something of an opéra bouffe with the cartoonist's rendering of the tow truck and the dying Democratic donkey as its cachet.[17] Attorney General McKittrick was also duly pilloried through a cartoon. Mrs. Richard Shewmaker, the Democratic wife of one of Forrest Donnell's Democratic counsel, summed up the anomaly: "After all, it was the Democrats who were in. If there was going to be any monkey business, they would do it."[18]

Mrs. Shewmaker's revulsion was shared by any number of leading Democrats: Governor Lloyd Stark, who had vetoed Joint Resolution No. 3, thereafter used his line-item veto to disapprove appropriation vouchers thereby bringing state business (including the legislators' pay) and the "investigation" to a standstill. Stark was joined by Democrats of the stature of state Senator Allen McReynolds and state senate majority leader, Phil Donnelly, as the ruling Democratic majority shattered on the rock of scandal. Nor did the General Assembly help matters. When the legislators caught sight of a black face in a group of St. Louis protestors in their gallery, the floor of the chamber exploded to shouts of "find him a cotton sack, we don't want any 10¢ votes."[19] Moreover, in a significant grass-roots rebellion, a number of counties refused to surrender their ballots, regardless of what Joint Resolution No. 3 commanded.

The dissident Democrats were joined by their seven copartisans of the solidly Democratic state supreme court that decisively resolved the mandamus and prohibition cases. The first judg-

16. *St. Louis Post-Dispatch*, January 14, 1941.

17. See *St. Louis Post-Dispatch*, November 18, 1940, January 2 and 25, 1941.

18. Depositional interview of Richard Shewmaker, February 17, 1986, Supreme Court of Missouri Historical Society, Jefferson City, Missouri.

19. "Legislators Shout and Boo," *St. Louis Post-Dispatch*, January 30, 1941.

ment came in the mandamus case on February 19, 1941; a unanimous court peremptorily ordered Speaker Osburn to do what the state constitution plainly ordered him to do—simply tabulate and proclaim the results on the basis of certifications previously furnished him. The next day the *Post-Dispatch* headline told the story: "Donnell Is Declared Elected by Speaker under Court Order."[20] And a Fitzpatrick cartoon entitled "The Majesty of the Law" supplied a felicitous epigraph of the controversy. Forrest Donnell was quietly inaugurated a week later by James Marsh Douglas, now chief justice. By singular irony, Douglas, a Pendergast target in the 1938 primary, not only administered the oath, but wrote the opinions of the court in the "Steal" cases.

The prohibition opinion was not handed down until June 21, the delay being occasioned by a postelectoral complication wherein McDaniel filed an orthodox recount petition on March 4. Under it, a new tabulation was begun whose preliminary findings confirmed Donnell's election and increased the latter's majority to seven thousand. On May 21, McDaniel conceded Donnell's election and withdrew his petition. The same day, the General Assembly discharged its own contest committee, causing the court to comment, "Because the people of Missouri attach supreme importance to the office of governor, it can be safely said that any such decisive action concerning a contest of this office which has been given such wide notoriety is well known to all persons . . . in this state."[21] Accordingly, the controversy in the prohibition action became pointless in the absence of any real disagreement, and the court dismissed the petition as the great governorship steal ended, not with a bang but with a whimper. It did not really end in a whimper because in consequence of the great governorship "steal" or otherwise St. Louis and Kansas City machines were in ruins by the end of the decade, and virtually all of the DeSoto conspirators had disappeared from Missouri's public life.[22]

The author of a trenchant description of the episode supplied an insightful closing note: "The voters were remarkably efficient

20. *St. Louis Post-Dispatch*, February 20, 1941.

21. State *ex rel.* Donnell v. Searcy, 152 S.W. 2d 8, 10 (Mo. en banc 1941).

22. Mayor Dickmann was defeated for reelection in the Spring municipal election of 1941. McKittrick defeated Senator Clark in the Democratic primary the previous year and lost to Donnell in the general election.

in punishing those responsible for the 'steal.' Generally, only those Democrats directly involved were defeated. Second, the role of the court demonstrates the importance we place on judicial judgment. A heated, partisan conflict with much at stake was ended by a single opinion. Parallels to Watergate can be overdone, but there are similarities."[23]

23. Thomas F. Soapes, "The Governorship 'Steal' and the Republican Revival in Missouri"; letter dated December 14, 1987, Thomas F. Soapes to the author.

26

Rat Alley

In the mid–1930s, a coterie of thugs from the hoodlum-ridden International Stagehands Union took over the St. Louis Local 143. Led by John "Big Nick" Nick and his associates, Clyde Weston and Congressman Edward "Putty Nose" Brady, the coterie terrorized the membership and then moved to shake down the movie-theater owners. In an early encounter with the owners, Brady observed that upon the payment of a sum of money a "satisfactory" 1936 wage contract might be negotiated. After a second meeting, which included hints that demands might include feather-bedding, the price went up to $7,500 and then to $10,000. The hat was accordingly passed among the owners who had deposited over $16,000 in a local bank. On October 16, 1936, Nick delivered a "no-raise" contract, which merely duplicated the 1935 agreement. The payoff occurred immediately afterward with Brady receiving $10,000 in large bills and driving off into the autumn evening.

Where the money went was problematical for by year's end Nick had shuffled business agents, appointing fellow hoodlum Weston to the office. Thereafter, Weston signed all union checks and treated the local's treasury as his own. More importantly he figured in a second payoff, receiving $6,500 from the cowed theater owners on Thanksgiving eve 1937 as the price of extending the "sweetheart" contract for yet another year. Both times Nick discreetly distanced himself from the actual payoff.

TWO LAWSUITS

Prompted by disclosures made by the *St. Louis Post-Dispatch*, nineteen veterans of Local 143 screwed up their courage and filed suit in January 1939 to oust Nick and break the union's control of their group. Within days of the members' suit, circuit attorney Franklin Miller persuaded the grand jury to indict Nick, Brady, and Weston for extortion. Nick and Brady were charged together on the 1936 $10,000 payoff, and Nick and Weston were similarly linked on the 1937 $6,500 one. The trials for both civil and criminal wrongdoing inched forward in the Circuit Court of St. Louis. The extortion cases were calendared in division 12, while the ouster action was set in division 2 in another building. Judge Oakley held a preliminary proceeding in division 2 almost immediately. He summarily expelled Nick and his henchmen and placed Local 143 in receivership. In October 1939, Nick took advantage of a contemporary "severance" rule, which prevented a jointly accused defendant from being tarred with the same brush used to incriminate a codefendant, and demanded and received a separate trial on the 1936 shakedown involving himself and Brady. After a series of false starts, Nick's case finally came on for trial in division 12 in January 1940. There the respected Judge Robert Aaronson found that the state had failed to prove beyond all reasonable doubt and to a moral certainty two critical elements of the extortion case against Nick: conspiracy and coercion. An acquittal was directed.

March opened with both the ouster and extortion trials coming on for final decision. On March 4, the extortion case against Brady was called before Judge Thomas Rowe, Jr., now presiding in division 12. In response to the judge's inquiry, circuit attorney Miller indicated his evidence would substantially duplicate the evidence presented in the earlier trial that acquitted Nick. Judge Rowe "quite properly" (as the supreme court later found) dismissed the case against Brady.

Twenty-four hours later in division 2, Judge Ernest Oakley illustrated the difference between criminal and civil standards of proof when he reached the conclusion that Nick had indeed gotten the money in the 1936 shakedown. Oakley issued a final decree in the ouster suit, ordering the $10,000 turned over to Local 143.

The distinction between a preponderance of evidence and evidence beyond a reasonable doubt failed to impress the editorial room of the *Post-Dispatch*. The day after the Brady dismissal, the lead editorial proclaimed the trials "A Burlesque in Justice" and continued in a satiric, theatrical theme: "The amazing case of Putty Nose, a legal skit in one very short act, presented under the auspices of the State of Missouri in association with the people of St. Louis in Circuit Court Criminal Division with the following cast: Putty Nose: State Representative Edward M. Brady . . . Judge Thomas J. Rowe, Jr." The next day, the successful ouster suit brought the full fusillade of the *Post*'s outrage in an even more pungent editorial: "Judge Rowe: Turn'em Loose"; "Judge Oakely: These Men Are Guilty."[1]

Accompanying the acid-penned ridicule of the seemingly inconsistent decisions was Daniel Fitzpatrick's cartoon "Burlesque House in Rat Alley." It was not reproduced in the official reports of the Missouri Supreme Court when the case got there, and Judge Charles Hays in writing the ultimate opinion provided a necessarily inadequate description of the artist's slashing, black-and-white style that purported

> to represent a burlesque theater in the city slums and entitled "Burlesque House in Rat Alley." The sign on the marquee of the theater is "10 grand gone with the wind" and some of the remarks apparently coming from the theater are "Ladies and gents, this performance opens wit' th' blessings of the law an 'th' courts!" and "Ain't severance wunnaful?" While one member of the waiting crowd is represented as saying "Who does th' strip tease?" and another replies "Nick does th' strip and Putty Nose does th' tease."[2]

Son of a lawyer and a member of a numerous and upwardly mobile Irish family, Judge Rowe was a pleasant and easy-going man who doubtless felt that he spoke the truth when he later told a *Post* reporter: "Don't get the idea there was anything personal in this. . . . I have no animosity. . . . If this were a matter against Tom Rowe personally, I could forget the whole thing, laugh it off and

1. "A Burlesque in Justice," *St. Louis Post-Dispatch*, March 5, 1940; "These Men Are Guilty," *St. Louis Post-Dispatch*, March 6, 1940.
2. "These Men Are Guilty," *St. Louis Post-Dispatch*, March 6, 1940

"Burlesque House in Rat Alley." *St. Louis Post-Dispatch*, photograph courtesy of State Historical Society of Missouri, Columbia.

go on. But what was done against the court, and as an elected officer of the people, I can't let it go unchallenged."[3]

Rowe never specifically mentioned the cartoon, which he saw for the first time on March 7, 1940, when he bought his paper. But unquestionably that was what really stung far beyond the ("Judge Rowe: Turn'em loose") editorial; as Rowe said, "To put [my] court in Rat Alley" understated his sense of outrage.[4] Fitzpatrick had been using the "Rat Alley" motif for years, and the dreary, rubbish-strewn thoroughfare, which could have been in the ghetto or on the riverfront, was one of the best-known locales in town. Rowe's anger at the paper would have been even more intense had he known that the locale of the *Post's* protest was the brainchild of its publisher, Joseph Pulitzer II, for which cartoonist Fitzpatrick duly thanked his boss.

In any event, it was but the work of a moment for Rowe to order circuit attorney Franklin Miller, whose offices were on the same floor as his court, to issue a citation against the paper itself, its managing editor, Ben Reese, its editorial page editor, Ralph Coghlan, and its cartoonist, Daniel Fitzpatrick, to show cause why they should not be punished for contempt of court. On March 18, Pulitzer, flanked by his three staffers, appeared in division 12. Resolution of the controversy was set for a few days later. Publisher and employees all asserted the *Post's* position, denying any animus against Judge Rowe but insisting on the *Post's* right to serve the public interest by free comment. Sitting in the court room audience, unnoticed, was *Post* staffer Irving Dillard, whom *Time* magazine pronounced the actual author of the offensive editorials.[5]

THE LAW OF THE CASE

Both sides feverishly prepared for the decisional hearing. The *Post* attorneys, John Raeburn Green and J. Porter Henry, were regular counsel for the paper and its radio station, KSD. They were assisted by Jacob Lashly, former ABA president and king of the St.

3. Memorandum from C. W. O'Malley to Joseph Pulitzer et al., Joseph Pulitzer II Papers, Library of Congress (hereafter cited as Pulitzer Papers).

4. *Id.*

5. *Time,* April 15, 1940.

Louis Bar, and Lashly's young partner, Clark M. Clifford, already showing signs of the brilliance that would bring national stature. On the other side stood circuit attorney Franklin Miller and volunteer William Gentry, an old-fashioned country lawyer who had moved to St. Louis from Columbia. Gentry, a stickler for courtroom decorum, was a brother of North Todd Gentry, onetime member of the Missouri Supreme Court.

While the legal talent seemed clearly on the side of the *Post*, the law of the matter was not. Back in 1903, the Missouri Supreme Court in an original proceeding had slapped down the *Warrensburg Standard Herald* for asserting that the supreme court had "sold" its judicial soul "to the corporations." Writing the opinion of the court, Judge William Champe Marshall of St. Louis replicated the sonority and style of his distant cousin and namesake, the great Chief Justice of the United States, in upholding the power of an offended judge to act as judge and jury and punish without limitation any contempt exhibited toward the court and its processes. Marshall pitched his case on Sir William Blackstone's concern lest courts lose "that regard and respect . . . so necessary for the good order of the kingdom."[6] Moreover, Marshall had held that this authority was vested in the judicial arm of the state by its original 1820 constitution and hence was beyond constraint by either legislative regulation or parallel constitutional guaranties of jury trial and freedom of the press. Even though committed outside the presence of the court and without immediate effect on proceedings therein, the potential for mischief was constructively implicit in any defamation of the judicial process.

Against this threatening backdrop, the *Post*'s defense was mounted with due regard to the court of public opinion wherein a newspaper trial of the judge himself was considered, including the use of a photograph of Rowe, described by a staffer as a "very hard and tough-looking customer."[7] The issue itself was tried on March 19, 1940, the Thursday preceding the coldest Easter in forty-six years. Circuit attorney Miller, emphasizing that he was speaking for Rowe himself, presented his evidence, which largely

6. State *ex inf.* Crow v. Shepherd, 76 S.W. 79, 84 (Mo. en banc 1903); William Blackstone, *Commentaries on the Law of England*, 4 vols. (1765), 285.

7. Memorandum from Ralph Coghlan to Joseph Pulitzer, March 11, 1940, Pulitzer Papers.

rested on the self-evidently defamatory content of the editorials
and cartoon. He was followed by Gentry, who hammered hard on
the Blackstone thesis that the issue concerned, not Judge Rowe's
sensibilities, but the integrity of the trial process itself.

The court had also sought additional counsel to present its
case; although the official minutes are silent, Judge Rowe reportedly attended a monthly meeting of the Executive Committee of
the St. Louis Bar Association to rally counsel for his cause where
only one dissident voice (Walston Chubb) was raised against the
issue of censorship. Judge Rowe had a heart condition, and he
was doubtless startled when the goateed Gentry orated in classic
Boone County style: "If your honor should die this moment, this
case would go on. It is not for your person nor for your single court,
but the dignity of all courts that is involved."[8] (Reportedly, Judge
Rowe also unsuccessfully sought a grand jury indictment against
the *Post* for criminal libel.)

In response, Clifford and Lashly rang the changes on the issue
of fact (the editorial-cartoon did not assail Judge Rowe personally)
and constitutionality (freedom of the press). Unmentioned was
the point that ultimately won the case and that was later suggested by young Milton Goldstein, a cub associate of John Green.
Goldstein was fresh out of the Harvard Law School where he had
attended the last courses taught by Felix Frankfurter prior to the
latter's appointment to the U.S. Supreme Court. The association
yielded an encounter with Frankfurter's longstanding hostility
toward constructive contempt, an attitude itself based on the historical research of Sir John Fox, a British legal scholar. Sir John
had discovered that the doctrine of unlimited judicial power to
punish contempt rested on a historical solecism, namely, an
unbelievable gaffe by Sir William Blackstone, who had cited a
nugatory opinion in an abandoned case to hold what it did not. To
be sure, contempt was punishable as any other crime, but only
after customary procedural safeguards of indictment and jury
trial. Moreover, punishment lay only for interference with a pending case but never as to a comment on a concluded one.

Judge Rowe took the arguments under advisement, and on
April 13, 1940, delivered his judgment. It came in time for the

8. *St. Louis Post-Dispatch*, March 20, 1940.

home edition of the principal defendant: *"Post-Dispatch* Found Guilty of Contempt: 2 Men Sentenced to Jail."[9] Beneath the headline appeared a photograph of the "criminals" Ralph Coghlan (twenty days and $200) and Daniel Fitzpatrick (ten days and $100). The *Post* itself was fined $2,000, and the charge against managing editor Reese was dismissed. The miscreants were pictured with an impishly grinning Sheriff James J. "Jimmy" Fitzsimmons under the caption, "In Durance Vile." The caption was sheer hyperbole, for the durance consisted in being served Coca-Cola by a lissome Mary Alice Quinn, the sheriff's secretary. ("Was she a blonde?" correctly inquired the sheriff's distant cousin and onetime law dean Paul Fitzsimmons, who searched his memory a half century after the event.)[10] Sheriff Fitzsimmons then took his prisoners to lunch at public expense while awaiting the formalities of release on bail.

The release was unusual because Judge Rowe refused to allow the conventional preliminaries for an appeal after reading his findings and punishments. Lashly and Clifford were accordingly forced to seek redress in the original, as distinguished from the appellate, jurisdiction of the state supreme court. Armed with a certified copy of the judgment, they departed by car for Jefferson City to request writs of habeas corpus and certiorari from Chief Justice Leedy, who handled such matters while the court was in vacation. Judge Leedy, thanks to widespread publicity, was not unprepared for his visitors. The custom in those days was for the presiding judge to take action on such an application after assembling the court en banc or getting the views of four of its seven members. Probably Leedy used the telephone to pursue the latter course for almost as soon as the applications were filed, a telegram went forward to Judge Rowe: "I am directed by the Court to request you to take no further action in the case of Franklin Miller, Circuit Attorney against Pulitzer Publishing Co. until the Court has passed upon petition for certiorari filed today. E. F. Elliott, Clerk."

The wire effectively stayed Judge Rowe's action; the paperwork was completed, and the prisoners were released at 4:50 P.M.

9. *Id.*, April 13, 1940.
10. Interview, Paul Fitzsimmons, October 27, 1987.

after six hours durance and were back at work the next morning. The wire also was something of a portent; in fact, signs abounded marking the decline of the unlimited-judicial-punishment doctrine for constructive contempt and its inconsistency with basic democratic values. These included the sheer unfairness of a pretrial "show cause" determination, lack of a jury trial, and, worse yet, determination of guilt by a judge already smarting under the sting of insult. Moreover, on a constitutional level, the U.S. Supreme Court was already considering for review two California cases wherein Harry Bridges and the *Los Angeles Times-Mirror* trashed judges far worse than the *Post-Dispatch* ever did.

Indeed, the Missouri Supreme Court had already indicated dissatisfaction with *Shepherd.* Six years after its pronouncement, the court split 4–3 on its application, and the great Henry Lamm, who had gutted the doctrine of constructive contempt with characteristic felicity of style, dissented forcibly: "The courts of Missouri need no such show of autocratic power; that they, in the future as in the past, may more surely build their dignity and usefulness solidly on the intelligent respect of the good citizen . . . than to build it on a show of wielding an uncontrollable power to fine and imprison."[11]

Other signs of the supreme court's discontent were not wanting in the official reports, but nevertheless *Shepherd,* bent perhaps but not broken, stood firm as what lawyers call the law of the case. It seemed impregnable against the expressions of sympathy that poured in to the *Post* from local competitors, St. Louis academicians, and distinguished out-of-town newsmen, like William Allen White and Colonel Robert McCormick. Even from the nation's capital correspondent Charles Ross wrote of the "great interest" justices Felix Frankfurter and Harlan Stone had expressed at a Washington dinner party. Ross passed on Frankfurter's surmise that the Missouri case might well wind up before the U.S. Supreme Court, so Ross "should tell them no more."[12]

The possibility of what would happen to *Shepherd* should the Supreme Court get its hands on the doctrine of constructive con-

11. Chicago, B & Q R.R. v. Gildersleeve, 118 S.W. 86, 96 (Mo. en banc 1909) (Lamm, J., dissenting).

12. "C. G. R." (Charles G. Ross) to Joseph Pulitzer, March 22, 1940, Pulitzer Papers.

tent came from U.S. District Judge Caskie Collet, a former member of the Missouri Supreme Court, then on temporary duty with the U.S. Court of Appeals. Judge Collet reported that his colleagues on that bench "were unanimous that the *Shepherd* case is 'cock-eyed' and that the United States Supreme Court will not only take jurisdiction of an appeal but will reverse it." However, Judge Collet also surmised that his former state colleagues would follow *Shepherd* and deny the *Post*'s plea. A resident of Jefferson City in daily touch with members of the court, Collet refused to give specifics for his conclusion but said only that he had "good and sufficient reason" for it.[13]

The three consolidated cases were argued October 8, 1940, with double time being set aside for the occasion. Lashly, Green, and J. Porter Henry argued for the *Post*, and Gentry, John Gilmore, and Louis Sher for the sheriff. The ACLU and the Missouri Press Association presented amicus briefs but were not permitted to speak. Oral argument was fought out on the evidentiary, constitutional, and policy bases of the *Post*'s appeal. Thrown into the brief, almost as an afterthought, was the historical infirmity of *Shepherd* suggested by Goldstein, who like the ACLU and the Missouri Press Association did not raise his voice in the courtroom but went to Jefferson City for the ride.

No minutes are published of the conferences of the Missouri Supreme Court, nor are the judges disposed to talk or write to outsiders about what goes on there. Moreover, even as the argument was reported in the *Post* for the same day, the story was silent on questions from the bench that might suggest which way the court was leaning. But the difficulty the court had in reaching its decision and overcoming the opposition of two of the strongest-minded judges of the court can be gleaned from the long interval that passed between submission of the case in early October and the decision of the court the following June. To be sure, there were other developments that slowed the decision—the bitter Democratic primary of the summer of 1940 and the equally turbulent "governorship steal" of early 1941 were obvious distracting factors. While awaiting a ruling, Green wrote the counsel in

13. Unsigned, undated, confidential memorandum from "Wieb" to Joseph Pulitzer, Pulitzer Papers.

the California contempt proceedings that the Missouri Supreme Court was not as prompt as that of the United States in handing down opinions, and that in this matter, the court might have some disposition to await the result of the California case before it ruled on the *Post-Dispatch*. Hence, it can only be surmised how the final *Post-Dispatch* judgment was hammered out sentence by sentence in an opinion that sought to amass a unanimous court behind the pronouncement. Authored by Judge Charles Hays, the opinion steered between the unlimited right of editorial defamation sought by the *Post* and the obvious necessity of keeping the judicial process free of outside influence.[14]

The critical pivot, accordingly, turned out to be the Blackstone blunder, the dictum supplied by Sir John Fox through Milton Goldstein: that courts did *not* have "since time immemorial" an inherent right to punish summarily for any statement that tended to subvert their process. Moreover, whatever had been the case in 1765 (the publication year of Blackstone's commentaries) courts had no such power in 1607, the cut-off date selected in Missouri's adoption of the English common law. The point was not mentioned before Rowe but was included as a subpoint in the brief Goldstein and Green wrote on appeal. A brilliant stroke, it cut the judicial issue to manageable size and reduced the contempt power to dealing with disruptive behavior in a *pending*—not *concluded*—case. The sole issue before the supreme court, accordingly, was whether the undeniably insulting cartoon and editorials could be fairly construed as referring to the Nick indictments for the 1937 shakedowns, which were still pending in Rowe's court, rather than the Nick-Weston extortion charge (1936) concluded with the dismissal of charges against the defendants. As Hays put it:

> The reason why a direct interference with a pending case is punishable is obvious. The trial cannot be stopped while another jury is impanelled and the interferers prosecuted criminally or sued civilly. The court must have the power to quickly and in summary fashion enforce its orders and prevent acts which would hinder and delay the pro-

14. State *ex rel*. Pulitzer Publishing Co. v. Coleman, 152 S.W. 2d 640 (Mo. en banc 1941).

ceeding before it. But in the case of a publication having reference to a closed case, these reasons do not exist.[15]

Judge Hays was unable to bring the entire court to concur in his reasoning, but they joined his result. Judges James Douglas and George Ellison stood fast on the proposition that, however Blackstone might have erred, "scandalizing the court"[16] (not the case here) could be actionable contempt. They joined in an opinion that concurred in the judgment, but as Goldstein later pointed out, dissent would have been more logical.

Nonetheless, the Ellison-Douglas concurrence was blurred into the larger picture when the *Post*'s Jefferson City correspondent wired his publisher on June 10, 1941: "State Supreme Court today unanimously decided in favor of the *Post-Dispatch* in contempt case. All sentences and fines reversed, and *Post-Dispatch*'s contentions completely upheld. Best regards." A jubilant *Post* headline exulted: "The *Post-Dispatch* Wins in Supreme Court Appeal on Rowe's Contempt Ruling."[17]

However, a subhead ("Decision in Post-Dispatch Case Broadens Right to Criticize Judge") did not reveal the narrow scope of the decision: free speech and free press concerned only past cases. The extension of protection to pending litigation had to await the action of the U.S. Supreme Court in the *Bridges* and *Times-Mirror* cases later in the year. Ironically, had the *Post* lost in Missouri, its appeal to Washington doubtless would have been consolidated with the latter cases with the Pulitzer name emblazoned not only on a great newspaper and a literary prize but also on landmark litigation.

TWO PICTURES

Nonetheless, the Missouri case was a victory for free speech and free press. Fitzpatrick provided a characteristic slashing black-and-white cartoon wherein an arm encased in judicial robe labelled "Missouri Supreme Court" held a pencil and wrote in bold script "Free Speech Upheld."[18]

15. *Id.* at 646.
16. *Id.* at 649.
17. Telegram from Lincoln Hockaday to Joseph Pulitzer, June 10, 1941, Pulitzer Papers; *St. Louis Post-Dispatch*, June 11, 1941.
18. *St. Louis Post-Dispatch*, June 11, 1941.

There was another picture. Coghlan wrote his boss of a request for it from the "golden-haired Hebe" alias Miss Quinn who had supplied Coca-Cola during the technical imprisonment: "Say, Mr. Coghlan, I don't want to be promiscuous, but would you let the Sheriff have copies of last Wednesday's paper in which his picture appeared?" Coghlan "after taking a moment to gulp over the 'promiscuous,'" gallantly responded "Certainly, Miss Quinn" and passed the request on to the publisher. With characteristic noblesse oblige, Pulitzer sent the requested photograph to Fitzsimmons "in token of my appreciation of the consideration and courtesy you showed Mr. Coghlan, Mr. Fitzpatrick, and myself while we were in your 'constructive custody.'"[19] Jimmy Fitzsimmons proved the urbanity was contagious when he acknowledged the gift: "The picture now adorns the wall of my office and has attracted many favorable comments for its excellent photography."[20]

TRAGIC ENDING

Judge Rowe supplied an ending to the case worthy of a Greek tragedy, for he went to his grave defamed and unvindicated. His selection as a Missouri delegate to the 1940 Democratic National Convention was characteristic of the political orientation of the Missouri judicial system. He went to the Chicago convention where he was found dead from a heart attack in a chair in the Sherman Hotel on the morning of July 17, 1940. His colleague Judge Coleman was substituted as the title defendant of the case, and Rowe, like Pulitzer, was denied the historical distinction of being personally named in the formal title of a landmark case in American legal history.

19. Memorandum from Ralph Coghlan to Joseph Pulitzer, April 11, 1940, Pulitzer Papers.

20. Undated letter from James T. Fitzsimmons to Joseph Pulitzer, Pulitzer Papers.

27

Civil Rights

The Gantt feud unquestionably was the product of personality differences among men doing difficult work in the hothouse atmosphere of court confidentiality. There were other reasons. One was the context of the times which caused the insurance rate litigation to go forward against a background of political upheaval and profound social change. An element in the latter mix was Missouri's racial situation, which not only shaped its law but also caused the state to become a crucible of constitutional controversy.

Blacks had been in the state from the very beginning of its modern history. The first had been brought by the French from Santo Domingo to work the lead mines, and they left little trace of themselves or their labors. More permanent was the arrival of free men of color (also from Santo Domingo). As hired men they accompanied the Laclede expedition that founded St. Louis and became the nucleus of the town's free black subcommunity. Their presence was substantially augmented by the great migration of the early nineteenth century when thousands of Americans, white and black, poured into the upper Louisiana Territory from the upper tier of the American South, and their sheer demographic presence irrevocably changed the territory, altering its everyday language and everyday law.

The black presence exerted a profound impact on the law and politics of the nascent state. Indeed, the response to that presence had almost aborted Missouri's admission to the Union (see chap. 2). The flashpoint had been a provision in the 1820 constitution that required the legislature to bar any free black from coming to or settling in the state "under any pretext whatsoever." The impasse was resolved by a requirement that the new state give assurance by solemn public act that the controversial provision would never be enforced so as to impair basic constitutional rights. Missouri complied somewhat sulkily, and its assurance was honored on paper for three decades. In 1847, however, and thanks to an incredible printer's error, Missouri found an excuse to repudiate its pledge and the offending exclusion phrase was written into law.[1]

Racial antipathy also underlaid the Jackson Resolutions of 1857 when the state legislature defiantly took its stand, ideologically at least, with the slave-holding South. Nonetheless beneath the surface, conditions belied the superficial tranquility. On Charles Dickens's visit to St. Louis in 1842, the distinguished author responded to assurances of slave contentment and docility with a sharp comment on the manifold ads in the newspaper seeking the whereabouts of runaways.

It took the upheaval of the Civil War to end slavery for good and for all. Limited local efforts at emancipation were undertaken by the 1861 convention. The coup de grace was delivered by the 1865 constitution and thirteen months later by the Thirteenth Amendment, authored by Senator John Brooks Henderson. Henderson was also a strong proponent of the Fifteenth Amendment, which gave the vote to black males. (As Virginia Minor's lawsuit pointed out, the right to vote for women of either race went unnoticed). Missouri's amended constitution of 1875 paralleled the Fifteenth Amendment and even went beyond it in recognizing and validating referenda that successively rejected and granted black suffrage. Not only did it ultimately enfranchise black males, but it restored former Confederates to the state voting rolls subject to a latent but subtle provision changing registration from a state to a local function.

While an even-handed concord was seemingly established, the

1. See Walter B. Stevens, *Centennial History of Missouri*, 581; H.R. 15th Leg., 1848 Mo. Laws 667. The law was part of a racist repression, which also forbade teaching slaves to read and write.

pace of events was undoing the balance. This was the rise of coerced racial separation, seemingly endorsed by Booker T. Washington's Atlanta speech of 1895 ("In all things that are purely
social we can be as separate as the fingers, yet one as the hand in
all things essential to mutual progress")[2] and the U.S. Supreme
Court's constitutional validation of the concept in the landmark
case of *Plessy v. Ferguson,* one year later.[3]

While segregation was an obvious advance over the dehuman-
izing brutality of slavery, the flaws in the remedy rather quickly
became apparent. One received its historical postmortem in the
Missouri Constitution of 1945: "No school district which permits
differences in wages of teachers having the same training and experience because of race or color, shall receive any portion of said
revenue or fund."[4] The constitutional sanction was necessitated
by the widespread practice of paying black teachers less than
whites of equal qualifications. From distant Tuskegee, Alabama,
Dr. Booker T. Washington scored the perverse compliment—that
black teachers because of presumed superiority could do the same
job as well as their white colleagues even when handicapped by
poorer facilities and lower pay. The practice was corrected in a
series of lower court cases and ended substantially by the leverage
of constitutional amendment. Parity in pay, however, was only
the beginning of the struggle for equal educational opportunity.
The latter was seen by virtually all black leaders as the indispensable beginning of their quest for equality.

A premature thrust at the heart of the problem came in 1890
out of Grundy County. The suit was itself remarkable in as much
as most civil rights litigation from *Catiche* and *Scott* to others
well into the twentieth century came out of St. Louis, thanks to
the matrix of an authentic black subcommunity and the relative
urbanity and tolerance of a big city. Nonetheless, it was a rural
black who attempted to strike down Missouri's separate but equal
school provisions, which had been provided in the 1865 constitution and continued in the 1875 successor. His complaint was

2. Carter Woodson, ed., *Negro Orators and Their Orations* (Washington,
D.C.: Associated Publishers, Inc., 1925), 580.
3. 163 U.S. 537 (1896).
4. Mo. Const. of 1945, art. IX, 3c.

that his children had to travel three-and-a-half miles to Trenton, Missouri, for their schooling while no white child in the district had to travel more than two. His specific complaint was that the practice was inconsistent with the command of the Fourteenth Amendment, which says that no state can deny "equal protection of the laws."

The Missouri Supreme Court turned him down cold, literally reading that segregation was commanded by the language of the current state constitution as mandatory: "Separate free public schools *shall* [emphasis mine] be established for the education of children of African descent."[5] Somewhat unctuously, this opinion approved the current system by arguing that "under it, the colored children of the state have made rapid stride in the way of educations, to the great gratification of every right-minded man."[6] As to the pivot of the decision the court simply cited *Roberts v. City of Boston*,[7] wherein the great Lemuel Shaw found a coerced separation constitutionally compatible with a requirement of equal protection of law.[8]

The overthrow of the *Roberts* case did begin on Missouri soil. The chain of causation had its origins when a black minister preached in St. Louis, meeting and ultimately marrying a young lady in the congregation. Their daughter in turn married a black Washington lawyer named Houston, and the child of that union laid the groundwork for the overthrow of the constitutionalized system of caste and color.

Charles Hamilton Houston was also a product of the establishment and had credentials therein—an Amherst Phi Beta Kappa key and a law review editorship at Harvard. He chose, however, to attack the establishment's caste system from the outside rather than profit from it within and did so as the dean of the Howard Law School in Washington, D.C. (A strategic position he later combined with the office of general counsel of the NAACP.) Thanks to his drive and charismatic personality, Houston transformed the Howard Law School from a sleepy, third-rate backwater into the West Point of the civil rights movement. There, carefully se-

5. Lehew v. Brummel, 15 S.W. 765, 765 (Mo. Div. 1 1891).
6. *Id.* at 766.
7. *Id.* at 767.
8. 59 Mass. (5 Cush.) 198 (1849).

lected young men were hammered into crack forensic advocates. The law school also served for Houston's command post, affording a panoramic view of a struggle against ingrained and institutionalized inequality. The inequality itself had many localized faces: educational, employment, and residential. Houston accordingly masterminded his scant resources into the most cost-effective encounter in the hope that one day the dragon of segregation would be brought down.

Houston's tactics were at the heart of a command decision that victory was possible only through the judicial process, not majoritarian politics. Hence, every lawsuit undertaken had to be fitted into a delicately balanced scheme of priorities. Education took on the foremost role for two reasons: First, without education, achievement of social and economic parity was impossible. Second, education, particularly graduate and professional education, offered an inviting target of least resistance, particularly alongside goals such as fair employment and fair housing.

An especially inviting target presented itself in the case of Lloyd Gaines, an honor graduate of Missouri's Lincoln University who sought admission to the School of Law at the University of Missouri. Missouri had met the need for black higher education with a two-pronged response: an all-black university, Lincoln, at Jefferson City, and payment of tuition at out-of-state schools for courses not offered at Lincoln. Gaines spurned the latter alternative, and predictably, his application for direct admission was turned down by the University Registrar, S. W. Canada, on the basis of the 1875 constitution.

"When I got over there," recollected St. Louis publisher Nathaniel Sweets, who accompanied Gaines to Canada's office, "the registrar saw me [and] said 'You must be in the wrong place.' The Gaines case had its beginning right in our little office."[9] On the very basis of that 1875 document—since Missouri provided neither separate, much less equal, legal education to black applicants—Gaines, backed by the NAACP, sued on January 24, 1936, to compel acceptance of his application through a writ of mandamus from

9. Nathaniel Sweets Interview, UMSL Oral History Program, St. Louis, Missouri.

the Circuit Court of Boone County. There were a few light moments when the case was tried. Dean William Masterson of the law school "wiggled like an angleworm" when grilled by Houston's relentless cross-examination on budgets, ratings, and parities, and suffered "an amazing lapse of memory."[10] There was little to be light-hearted about for in seeking admittance Gaines literally took his life in his hands. Just thirteen years earlier, a black janitor (James Harris) had been lynched on the campus in the presence of hundreds of students.[11] Predictably, the circuit court denied the writ, and Gaines appealed the refusal to the Supreme Court of Missouri. On December 9, 1937, that tribunal upheld the refusal, and Gaines sought review in the U.S. Supreme Court.[12]

The issue there had a narrow focus: did the provision for out-of-state tuition satisfy the command *Plessy v. Ferguson* that separate facilities be equal? In the context of the times, the question was a close one, and the answer depended on whether it was considered liberally or strictly. Chief Justice Charles E. Hughes considered it narrowly:

> The admissibility of laws separating the races in the enjoyment of privileges afforded by the State rests wholly on the equality of the privileges which the laws give to the separated groups within the State. . . . [Here] the white resident is afforded legal education within the State; the negro resident having the same qualifications is refused it there and must go outside the State to obtain it.

The chief justice then cast his thunderbolt "*That* [emphasis added] is a denial of the equality of legal right to the enjoyment of the privilege which the State has set up, and the provision for the payment of tuition fees in another State does not remove the discrimination."[13]

10. Genna R. McNeil, *Groundwork* (Philadelphia: University of Pennsylvania Press, 1983), 144.
11. See *New York Times*, April 30, 1923.
12. State *ex rel.* Gaines v. Canada, 113 S.W.2d 783 (Mo. en banc 1937).
13. Missouri *ex rel.* Gaines v. Canada, 305 U.S., 337, 349–50 (1938). Interestingly, notwithstanding protest of distinguished men like W. E. B. Du Bois ("that Capital 'N,'" crisis quoted in Lester, ed., *The Seventh Son: The Thought and Writing of W. E. B. Du Bois*, vol. 2, [1971], 12–13. "Negro" was lowercased in both the Missouri and U.S. reports).

INVISIBLE WALLS[14]

Houston's next great victory in the black quest for equality came a decade after *Gaines;* it also came out of Missouri and involved a judgment of its supreme court. While access to education was the almost self-evident priority in the civil rights agenda, housing was a close second. For one thing, it represented the fruits of equal employment opportunity. For another, freedom of choice in this area seemed indispensable to freedom of movement within the larger society. The one barrier here was the restrictive covenant, seemingly so time-tried and fire-tested as to be beyond litigational overthrow. Instrumentally, the covenant was a provision in a deed that covered a master plot whereby lease, sale, or occupancy of any property to blacks was forbidden. The prohibition was widely used and routinely enforced (by expulsion of the black occupier). The covenant had been constitutionally validated by the U.S. Supreme Court in *Corrigan v. Buckley*[15] and endorsed by the prestigious American Law Institute in their *Restatement of Property.* The *Corrigan* case held the seeds of its own destruction by asserting that the Fifth Amendment applied only to governmental action and did not touch individual effort. There was already a countering strain in the law: the Supreme Court had decided that a state could not ordain residential segregation, however much private parties might do so.

By the 1930s the fruits of the covenant were painfully obvious: "Negro-occupied sections of cities throughout the country were fatally unwholesome places, a menace to health, morals and general decency of cities and plague spots for race exploitation, friction and riots."[16] Such covenants were widespread in St. Louis, and one covered a modest residence at 4600 Labadie Avenue on the city's north side. The house was purchased by J. D. Shelley, hard-working and thrifty newcomer from Mississippi. The Shelleys moved in on October 9, 1945, and were served with a summons the next day in a lawsuit which sought to annul the transaction by reason of a restrictive covenant executed in 1911. The nominal

14. For this phrase I am indebted to my colleague Professor Leland Ware who has the title deeds thereto and uses it in "Invisible Walls: An Examination of the Restrictive Covenant Cases," 67 Wash. U. L. Q. 737 (1989).

15. 271 U.S. 323 (1926).

16. *Committee Report on Negro Housing* (Washington, D.C.: GPO, 1932), 46.

plaintiff, Kraemer, was actually the proxy of the Marcus Avenue Homeowners' Association.

After two days of hearings, the St. Louis Circuit Court dismissed the law suit, not on constitutional grounds but on Missouri real estate law. The covenant, so Judge Koerner ruled, was defective because it had not been signed by all the owners of property it purported to cover. The decision was promptly appealed to the Missouri Supreme Court. On December 9, 1946, that court reversed the decision.[17] Not all owners in the area were required to sign the covenant, the court held, but only those whose property was actually covered.

Even as it acknowledged the appalling state of the St. Louis ghetto as "bringing deep concern to everyone"[18] the court by Judge Douglas's opinion unanimously upheld the covenant. The Shelleys' local counsel, George Vaughn, responded on April 21, 1947, by requesting the United States Supreme Court to hear the case. The request was granted June 23, 1947. Vaughn's basis of appeal was that use of state courts to enforce covenants impermissibly crossed the line between public and private action.

There was some squabbling concerning coordinating the St. Louis case with covenant litigation in other cities and securing the favorable intervention via an amicus curiae brief from the Truman administration. Oral argument took place January 15 and 16 in 1948 before an abbreviated bench. Justices Jackson, Reed, and former St. Louisan Wiley Rutledge disqualified themselves, unquestionably because of their ownership or occupancy of covenanted residences—itself an index of the ubiquitous reach of the invisible walls in American life.

The decision came down on May 3, 1948, in *Shelley* and a Detroit companion case.[19] The chief justice of the United States, Fred Vinson, wrote the opinion, which did not outlaw covenants but held them unenforceable in court. The Missouri Supreme Court was reversed. Charles Houston had but a short time to savor his triumph. His weak heart gave way beneath his workload, and he died April 22, 1950, at age fifty-four.

17. Kraemer v. Shelley, 198 S.W.2d 679 (Mo. en banc 1946).
18. *Id.* at 683.
19. 334 U.S. 1 (1948).

PROSPECT

28

The Assault on the Citadel

Throughout its century and a half of existence, the Missouri Supreme Court by and large has been a symbol of stability and continuity in the law. Not given to judicial adventurism, it has been especially sensitive to the boundary between the legislative and the judicial function commanded by the constitution. It is particularly faithful to the injunction, "Dicere Non Dare Legem," ("To speak, but not to give the law"), which is carved in the stone over its entrance. Nonetheless, as Justice Holmes noted, all courts legislate in the very nature of the judicial process, the legitimacy depending on whether the judicial legislation is "molecular or molar"—small or large.[1]

There is another problem with judicial legislation. It is inevitably retroactive since such "laws" (if indeed judicial decisions are laws) go on and off the books without the forewarning inherent in the usual business of a legislative assembly. The results usually are embodied in an expectation that the created legal interest will continue, a circumstance that may well prompt the investment of money and could constitute a property right under constitutional protection.[2]

1. Southern Pacific Co. v. Jensen, 244 U.S. 205, 221 (1917).
2. Jackson v. Chew, 25 U.S. (12 Wheat.) 153 (1827).

HUMANITARIAN NEGLIGENCE

The virtue and vice of judicial legislation and the impact of new times and new cultural values was illustrated by the rise and fall of a unique Missouri legal institution, the so-called humanitarian doctrine. It was a variant of the rule of the last clear chance, itself a softening of the ancient common law dogma whereby the slightest negligence of the victim forfeited any claim of recovery against a careless wrongdoer. England itself had revolted against the rule of contributory negligence in 1842 by providing that even where the victim was himself negligent, a wrongdoer who had the last clear chance to avoid the accident was nevertheless liable for the physical injury and property damage his own carelessness had caused.

The "last clear chance" doctrine traditionally deals with the question of who *actually* caused the accident in terms of a victim who was in a position of *discovered* peril by reason of his own prior negligence or the wrongdoer who was guilty of immediate and remediable carelessness. In a subtle shift, Missouri moved the issue to *discoverable* peril, thereby penalizing the actual wrongdoer and excusing the almost equal carelessness of the victim.[3] In brief, the wrongdoer was penalized for negligently failing to discover the victim's negligence.

The early decisions were incorporated, almost unthinkingly, into a rule that permitted recoveries by victims whose responsibility for the accident barely fell short of suicidal intent. As the doctrine evolved, it contemplated difficult fact applications, Talmudist distinctions, and frequent injustice. It was persistently criticized.[4] A distinguished member of the Missouri Supreme Court privately observed that fourteen versions of the doctrine seemed to exist on a tribunal consisting of seven judges and six commissioners—a circumstance explainable only by the fact that one member held two personal versions.[5]

The doctrine got its name from the great Henry Lamm: "The

---

3. Kelly v. Hannibal & St. Joseph R.R., 75 Mo. 138 (1881).
4. See Glen A. McCleary, *The Bases of the Humanitarian Doctrine Reexamined*, 5 Mo. L. Rev. 56 (1940).
5. Orally to the author, October 29, 1986 (Judge James A. Finch, Jr.).

precepts of humanity—the tender regard every man must have for the life and limb of other men."[6] He also seemed to rivet the doctrine on the state by pronouncing it too deeply embedded to be overturned by anything save legislative act.[7]

As the years went by, both the humanitarian doctrine and the increasing dissatisfaction with it became engraved in judicial and legal attitudes. Beyond Missouri's borders the common law doctrines of negligence, contributory negligence, and last clear chance were increasingly supplanted by the common sense continental rule of comparative negligence. Under the latter rule any recovery of a victim was reduced in the proportion that his own perceived fault had contributed to his own misfortune. By 1983 forty states, Puerto Rico, and the Virgin Islands had adopted comparative negligence as the rule for accidental injury. Thirty-two jurisdictions had accepted it by statute, and eight by judge-made "law."

Increased dissatisfaction with humanitarian's minute factual distinctions and manifest injustices were summarized by William Prosser as a "floundering, haphazard, make-shift device," which applied to bicycle accidents a rule generated by railroad fatalities. Dissatisfaction culminated in 1977 with a call by the supreme court—on its own motion—for briefs and argument as to whether the humanitarian doctrine should be reexamined—and by necessary implication—should be changed.[8]

Change on the court's motion began the following year when on a different but related point of law the supreme court demolished the distinction between primary and remote negligence in a lawsuit by an injured railroad employee wherein the defendant employer sought to bring a boxcar manufacturer into the case as a coresponsible party.[9] Almost as it did so, the court reiterated its

6. See Dutcher v. Wabash R.R., 145 S.W. 63, 69 (Mo. en banc 1912); Murphy v. Wabash R.R., 128 S.W. 481, 485 (Mo. en banc 1910).

7. *Murphy*, 128 S.W. at 485.

8. William Prosser, "Comparative Negligence," 51 Mich. L. Rev. 465, 474 (1953); see also Epple v. Western Auto Supply Co., 557 S.W.2d 253 (Mo. en banc 1977).

9. Missouri Pacific R.R. v. Whitehead & Kales Co., 566 S.W.2d 466 (Mo. en banc 1978).

conviction that overthrow of the humanitarian doctrine was a matter for the legislature, not judges.[10]

Five times the court invited the legislature to act, and repeatedly the General Assembly declined by inaction. Finally, a reductio ad absurdum of the humanitarian doctrine's distinction appeared in a case out of St. Louis County involving a collision between an overtaking motorcycle and a car turning left. The focus of the controversy was whether the defendant motorist's reaction time— estimated by the injured motorcyclist as "a second"—was found by the St. Louis appeals court to be insufficient to establish the motorist's liability under the humanitarian rules established by the state supreme court.[11] The appellate court on its own motion transferred the case to Jefferson City where the chicken of the humanitarian doctrine had indeed come home to roost.

The appellate court tactfully suggested the evolving line of the superior tribunal's decisions had painted the law into a corner, obliterating all reasonable distinction between the humanitarian doctrine and last clear chance. The supreme court, quoting Dean Prosser, realized that it was impaled on a dilemma—that last clear chance shifted the entire loss to the defendant and that it was "no more reasonable to charge the defendant with the plaintiff's share of the consequences of his fault than to charge the plaintiff with the defendant's; and it is no better policy to relieve the negligent plaintiff of all responsibility for his injury than it is to relieve the negligent defendant."[12]

Dean Prosser's solution—to clear the decks and abolish last clear chance (and its wayward offspring, the Missouri humanitarian doctrine) in favor of a comprehensive system of comparative negligence[13]—involved the court in an even harder dilemma— whether to expropriate a judgment of $20,200 awarded the plaintiff under the law of Missouri as it stood on the date of his injury. This ex post facto action, always inherent in judicial legislation, would have raised serious questions under both state and federal constitutions had it been attempted by legislative act. Even had

---

10. Steinman v. Strobel, 589 S.W.2d 293, 294 (Mo. en banc 1979).
11. Gustafson v. Benda, 661 S.W.2d 11 (Mo. en banc 1983).
12. *Id.* at 13.
13. Prosser, *supra* n. 8 at 474.

the court made its judgment effective only as to accidents occurring after the judgment, serious problems of the logistics of effective date and the bedrock separation of powers would remain.

Nonetheless, the court bit the bullet, and on November 22, 1983, undertook a massive repudiation of its past and abolished the humanitarian doctrine in favor of comparative fault. Two judges dissented; Judge Billings concurred, setting out the bare bones of the matter in something of a confession of error: "Historically, contributory negligence, last clear chance, and humanitarian negligence were born by judicial decisions. By judicial decision we bury them."[14]

Doubtless one factor that spurred the court was the fact that for years juries had been discounting a victim's recovery by the amount his own negligence had contributed to the accident. In a sense the voice of the people had spoken and despite regrets by eminent scholars like Dean Griswold of Harvard, humanitarian negligence, Missouri's contribution to the law of personal injury, was indeed buried, probably to stay.[15]

THE ROOTS OF CHANGE

Judicial activism to create and then destroy the humanitarian doctrine was built into the Missouri legal system almost at the very moment the territorial legislature adopted the common law of England for their new jurisdiction. Indeed, the incremental revision of judge-made law had been strikingly shown by the work and opinions of one of the great judges of that court who masterfully balanced continuity and change. Two opinions graphically show Judge Laurance Hyde's mastery of this aspect of the art and craft of judging.

One came in *Hull v. Gillioz* where Hyde, then a commissioner, revised and extended the "attractive nuisance" doctrine.[16] That doctrine, like humanitarian negligence, was part of the progressive softening of the harsh strictures of the common law. Under the common law, a landowner owed no duty whatsoever to

14. *Gustafson*, 661 S.W.2d at 28.
15. See Griswold, *Law and Lawyers in the United States* (London: Stevens, 1964), 61; letter to the author, December 12, 1983.
16. 130 S.W.2d 623 (Mo. Div. 1 1939).

trespassers who entered his premises at their own risk. That harsh rule broke down in the case of children who were attracted to property by railroad turntables and were hurt after playing on the dangerous structures. In *Gillioz*, the little plaintiff was injured while playing on the defendant's premises by the fall of a heavy iron beam. The issue was squarely drawn: should the landowner's liability be limited to *inherently* dangerous instrumentalities, like a railroad turntable, or extended to situations just as dangerous perhaps but lacking the element of fascination and invitation? In a masterful performance Hyde opted for the injured toddler. Quoting Henry Lamm, Hyde found that the stacking of iron bars coupled with the landowner's knowledge of childish trespass produced landowner liability and so moved Missouri doctrine into the forefront of American law.

Hyde's other exemplar of common law flexibility came in the case of *Thatcher v. Lewis*, a controversy whose longevity more than rivaled the insurance rate litigation of the 1930s. The issue was the 1848 will of Bryan Mullanphy, which left his residuary estate to the city of St. Louis "to furnish relief to all poor immigrants and travellers coming to St. Louis on their way, bona fide, to settle in the West."[17] The amorphous bequest had been before the Missouri Supreme Court five times previously and had been noted in histories of the American West. By the mid-1930s, the surge of westward immigration had ceased, and the heirs at law of the bachelor testator resumed their attack to break the will.

Hyde brilliantly repelled them in an opinion that applied the ancient doctrine of cy pres—that the original intention of a benefactor will be carried out as nearly as possible except when original circumstances change. Here, Hyde applied the concept and resolved the controversy in a lucid and forceful statement of the key fact: "We think we can reasonably say that it was his probable intent . . . [that] the fund be used as long as the problem of travel might create conditions . . . which would require aid." Thus, judicial creativity afforded relief in a depression-beset city in a circumstance that a long-dead benefactor had never contemplated.

17. 76 S.W.2d 677, 678 (Mo. Div. 1 1934).

THE TRANSFORMATION

The quantum jump in the court's attitude was clearly apparent in 1969 with the decision in *Abernathy v. Sisters of St. Mary's*[18] wherein a virtually unanimous court abolished the venerable immunity of a charity for its negligence. Rooted in English law, the immunity had been adopted in Missouri by judicial decision in 1907. The doctrine rested on two bases: First, that a beneficiary of a private charity impliedly waived any claim he might have against it for the negligent misconduct of employees. Second, the assets of a charity constituted a trust fund dedicated only to being spent on the purposes for which the charity was founded.

Both were demolished in an opinion by Chief Justice Fred Henley that aborted charitable immunity out of hand as part of the common law of Missouri. Somewhat defensively, noting that the doctrine had been born of judicial decision and might be so put to rest, Henley did precisely that. Obviously uneasy over the court's sledgehammer approach, Judge Robert Donnelly concurred but preferred a case-by-case reexamination of fact situations in preference to total abolition.

The immediate consequences of the court's action were apparent in a dissenting opinion filed by Lester Cox, Springfield philanthropist-industrialist and alter ego of the Burge-Protestant Hospital. The dissent was filed, not with the clerk but with Cox's longtime friend and fellow curator of the University of Missouri, Judge James A. Finch, Jr.: "Jim, I think that opinion is the worst thing that could ever happen, and I'm surprised that someone from a small town would be guilty of such a stupid thing." Cox wrote well before the advent of medical malpractice superliability, but he put his finger on who would ultimately pay for the court's decision. "Jim, do you know what you have done to poor folks in hospital? . . . We will have to add 75 cents per head to pay for claims."[19]

Abernathy may well have crossed Holmes's line between molar and molecular judicial legislation. In any event, it had a context whereby venerable and seemingly settled precedent was facilely

18. 446 S.W.2d 599 (Mo. en banc 1969).
19. John Hulston to Paul Barrett, March 11, 1981, from copy supplied by Judge Barrett to the author.

revised by the court. Such turnabouts include (the list is illustrative and not determinative) *Virginia D. v. Madesco Inv. Corp.* and *Jackson v. Ray. Kruse Const. Co.*, which enlarged premises liability; *Bass v. Nooney Co.*, which abandoned the "impact" requirement in torts; and *Firestone v. Crown Center Development Corp.*, which abolished remittitur whereby courts could temper as extravagant jury verdicts.[20]

THE TIPPING POINT

The real mutational change in the Missouri Supreme Court came in the abolition of sovereign immunity in *Jones v. State Highway Commission*, which empowered victims of state agency negligence to sue for injury. In many ways the decision was an anticlimax; the real encounter came earlier in *O'Dell v. School District of Independence.*[21]

In *O'Dell* the real issue was whether the Missouri Supreme Court sat as a judicial tribunal or a constitutional convention. The battle was fought out on the issue of whether a school district was liable for the negligence of an employee who injured a pupil. Judges Donnelly and Finch served as surrogates to fight out the principal issue in powerful and memorable presentations. The confrontation took the pair back to the adoption of the common law of England by the territorial legislature in 1816 and well beyond that benchmark to what the courts of England had to say on the issue long before Missouri was a state or had even been thought of.

There was an especial nuance: Did the "reception" statute of 1816 enable Missouri courts to revise or reject decisions that had proved mistaken or improvident in the same way that British courts, or, conversely, did the passage of time and the reiteration of sovereign immunity by repeated decisions of the Missouri Supreme Court so ingrain the doctrine as to require, constitutionally, its repeal by legislative act as the only legitimate mode of law making by a self-governing people?

Judge Finch presented the case for repeal in an opinion of un-

---

20. 648 S.W.2d 881 (Mo. en banc 1983); 708 S.W.2d 664 (Mo. en banc 1986); 646 S.W.2d 765 (1983); 693 S.W.2d 99 (Mo. en banc 1985).
21. 557 S.W.2d 225 (Mo. en banc 1977); 521 S.W.2d 403 (Mo. en banc 1975).

characteristic length but typical power. He first attacked the moral underpinnings of the doctrine as an insensible anachronism embodying the very idea (that the King could do no wrong) which sent the American colonists into rebellion. He also appealed to the common law, which Missouri had adopted in 1816, that contemplated judicial revision of judge-made rules which had proved inadequate under new social conditions.

Judge Donnelly and sovereign immunity prevailed, but victory was both temporary and short-lived; so was the reversal of the victory. The climate of the times and burgeoning judicial activism produced a reversal in *Jones* as soon as new appointments changed the composition of the court. Judge Donnelly and the old order were vindicated as the legislature reversed the *Jones* holding and reinstituted sovereign immunity in the shortest order thereafter.

29

Sunset and Evening Star

Judge Donnelly's bitter dissent in *Jones* was an accurate index of the mutational change in the character and function of his court: "Until today we enjoyed a system of government in Missouri in which the judicial department did not presume to legislate public policy."[1]

Perhaps the judge protested too much. From the very beginning the court had been intervening in public policy. Thus, its veto of the stay law legislation of 1821 adopted (somewhat uneasily to be sure) the Marshall doctrine of judicial review without a single explicit word of constitutional authorization (see chap. 3). An even more blatant example of judicial adventurism came in the first *Dred Scott* case where a massive repudiation of the court's own precedent was undertaken solely to manipulate a point of view in a national political controversy (see chap. 10). Cut from the same cloth was the court's validation of the ouster of the judges by a bench that had taken—without a qualm—the oath at which Father Cummings balked (see chap. 12); likewise its recalcitrant attitude toward monopoly and industrial accidents must be noted.

Jones, however, was something else again in possibly crossing the line which separated the legitimate from the illegitimate, exemplifying T. S. Eliot's graceful insight: "The last temptation is

1. Jones v. State Highway Comm'n, 557 S.W.2d 225, 231 (Mo. en banc 1977).

the greatest treason: / To do the right deed for the wrong reason."[2]
Judge J. P. Morgan, concurring in *O'Dell*, explained how the line
"to do the right thing for the wrong reason" was crossed by attempted judicial intermeddling in the expenditure and disposition of tax-raised funds.

Indeed, as Alexander Hamilton wrote in the *Seventy-fourth
Federalist*, severance of the authority of the purse and the sword
from the judiciary was indispensable to the separation of powers
and the keystone of the constitutional balance.

Perhaps it was too much to expect that Missouri could stand
apart from the wave of constitutional change sweeping the republic in the unrest following the social upheaval of the middle 1960s.
Gone was the disposition to tolerate short-run injustices in the
hope of long-term correction. The impatience of the body politic
communicated itself to the bench and with it the view that the
judiciary should take the lead in social reform should the political branches fail to act. The new attitude was totally subversive
of the framers' intention to build the firewalls of separation between the components of political power and disabling any branch
of government from exercising any power entrusted to the others.
In particular did the new revisionism destroy the Hamiltonian
perception of the impartial judge who exercised only judgment
but never will. Thus there arose the disposition to see a cure for
every social ill in some constitutional "principle," which impelled
the judiciary to assume general governmental powers. This disposition, called by Caesar Rodney "the leprosy of the bench,"[3] had
infected the Supreme Court of the United States and virtually
everyone of the high state judiciaries.

Missouri had been virtually the last to succumb. Even at this
stage the troublesome admonition of Mr. Justice Harlan applies
with special force:

The Constitution is not a panacea for every blot upon the public welfare, nor should this Court, ordained as a judicial body, be thought of as

2. *Murder in the Cathedral*, Part I, in T. S. Eliot, *Complete Poems and
Plays* (1909–1950; reprint, San Diego: Harbrace, 1971), 196.

3. Caesar Rodney to Thomas Jefferson, October 31, 1808; Warren, *The
Supreme Court in United States History*, 3 vols. (Boston: Little, Brown, 1924),
1:624–25.

a general haven for reform movements. The Constitution is an instrument of government, fundamental to which is the premise that in a diffusion of governmental authority lies the greatest promise that this Nation will realize liberty for all its citizens. This Court, limited in function in accordance with that premise, does not serve its high purpose when it exceeds its authority, even to satisfy justified impatience with the slow workings of the political process.[4]

There is another side to the coin: throughout its history the Missouri Supreme Court has been an activist tribunal, using its inherent constitutional authority with decisiveness and vigor. Virtually all the real estate law in the state is a product of judicial effort; something of the same genre came in the establishment of its Judicial Council in 1934. The body consisted of eleven members, nine appointed by the court with the chairmen of the judiciary committees of the upper and lower house of the General Assembly. The council was established by the court on its own motion without legislative authorization and was generally charged with surveillance of the administration of justice in Missouri and making recommendations for improvement.[5]

Here also must be noted the contemporary establishment by the court of an advisory committee, which transferred attorney discipline from volunteer to an institutionalized basis. Even more important in marking the maturity of the court was the institution of MAI (Missouri Approved Instructions), which speeded trials, expedited appeals, and created a veritable *corpus juris* of state law.

In the mid-1940s the court, again on its own motion and under its rule-making power, integrated the state's bar, requiring all licensed attorneys to join and to pay an enrollment fee. The legitimacy and limits of judicial power were again approached when some two decades later the court imposed continuing legal education as a retroactive condition of licensing, thereby forcing adults to sit as schoolchildren during droning lectures by law professors and putative experts.

IMPERIALIZATION

One development in the transformation of the court came in the mid-1960s. A cultural historian might see great significance in

4. Reynolds v. Sims, 377 U.S. 533, 624–25 (1963) (Harlan, J., dissenting).
5. Supreme Court Rule 39, 334 Mo. xix–xx.

the adoption of robes by a court that had up to that time sat in business suits. The sartorial change had been delayed by the obdurate resistance of Judge S. P. Dalton: "They'll never get one on me."[6]

A parallel datum was the use of clerks, whereby two bright young law graduates were assigned to each member of the court for assistance in research, opinion-writing, and the like. Doubtless the institution of the clerkships had an element of necessity due to the phaseout of the commissionerships. Nonetheless, the two developments, providing both raiment and retinue to the judges, could be perceived as an appropriate symbolization of the subtle transformation of the judiciary from members of a court of review to the guardians of platonic guided democracy.

The disintegration of the old order was even more strikingly shown in the area of substantive law. An ominous, dark shadow loomed over not only the principle of stare decisis but more enduring values suggested by the one-vote margin that prohibited death by dehydration of an unwanted and comatose patient. Cut from the same cloth was the decision suggesting that a landlord was liable in civil damages for the rape of a tenant (see chap. 20).

The critical center of that tension provided the matrix of the controversy over judicial review *versus* judicial supremacy. The distinction has been neatly summarized by a leading scholar:

> It [is] one thing to say that the Supreme Court might refuse to enforce a law plainly in conflict with a specific provision of the Constitution. It [is] another thing to say that the Court was the final, authoritative arbiter of all questions involving the interpretation of the Constitution. The distinction is between the institution of judicial review, narrowly defined, and the doctrine of judicial supremacy or judicial sovereignty which did not become settled American dogma until the twentieth century.[7]

From the very time the Missouri Supreme Court engaged the question, it had opted, albeit uneasily, for judicial supremacy (see chap. 3). Down the years, some voices of distinction have been heard in opposition. Abraham Lincoln's assertion that—despite his constitutional objection to the spread of slavery—he would

---

6. Personal recollection by the author of Judge Paul Barrett's comment about Judge Dalton.

7. Don E. Fehrenbacher, *The Dred Scott Case*, 440.

not free Dred Scott if he could was an especially nuanced and subtle dissent. For more blunt and direct was Andrew Jackson's bristling disagreement that every American who swears to support the Constitution does so as he understands it, not as a court understands it.

Moreover, the supporting arguments are especially unconvincing. Hugo Black's sunset adherence after a lifetime of doubt simply asserted that in the vagaries of providence, things somehow came out all right.[8] Learned Hand, who overcame the absence of a single authorizing word in the constitutional text by asserting that judicial supremacy was a precondition of success, simply substituted a sonorous ambiguity for rational explication.

DEATH BY DEHYDRATION

The conflict between the old and the new came to the court in *Cruzan*. The court overturned its judgment and directed employees of a state hospital to withhold nutrition and hydration from a patient in a persistent vegetative state without realistic hope of recovery.[9] The Jasper County probate court had entered this de facto death sentence on the basis of the patient's right to liberty, due process, and equal protection under both state and federal constitutions. Indeed, the legislature had already spoken to the point and set death standards on the basis of national norms of respiration, circulation, and brain function.[10]

The majority opinion written by Judge Edward Robertson, Jr., noted: "This case presents a single issue for resolution: May a guardian order that food and water be withheld from an incompetent ward who is . . . alive within the meaning of [the statute] and not terminally ill?"[11] Omitted was Judge Lamm's earlier citation of Blackstone as part of Missouri law: "There is a primary maxim of the law that in favor of life, liberty, and innocence, all

8. Gerald T. Dunne, *Hugo Black* (New York: Simon & Schuster, 1977), 414.
9. Cruzan v. Harmon, 760 S.W. 2d 408 (Mo. en banc 1988).
10. Mo. Rev. Stat. 194.005 (1986).
11. *Cruzan*, 760 S.W.2d at 412. The decision was ultimately affirmed by the U.S. Supreme Court: Cruzan v. Missouri Dept. of Health, 497 U.S. 261 (1990). After a second hearing, purporting to comply with the standards of existing law, support was ended. At 3 A.M. on the day after Christmas 1990, Ms. Cruzan died of thirst.

things are to be presumed." Judge Robertson noted that "what is really at stake" is that the state of Missouri "make Nancy die by starvation and dehydration."[12] His opinion refused to align Missouri with the majority of states that had considered the question: "The state's concern with the sanctity of life rests on the principle that life is precious and worthy of preservation without regard to its quality. This latter concern is especially important when considering a person who has lost the ability to direct her medical treatment."[13]

Three dissenters saw no such principle. Judges Blackmar, Welliver, and Higgins rejected the absolutist view in favor of a revisionist ethic that appraised life on the basis of quality rather than biology. Moreover, Judge Welliver focused on the razor-thin margin being effected by the vote of a nonmember of the permanent court.[14] Indeed, the state of the thing might well have been captured by William Butler Yeats: "Turning and turning in the widening gyre / The falcon cannot hear the falconer / Things fall apart; the center cannot hold."[15]

12. *Cruzan*, 760 S.W 2d at 412.

13. *Id.* at 419.

14. At the time there was one vacancy on the court, and the six regular members were divided. Judge James Reinhard of the Eastern District of the Court of Appeals was designated as a special judge for the case.

15. William B. Yeats, "The Second Coming," quoted from John Bartlett's *Familiar Quotations*, 15th ed. (Boston: Little, Brown, 1988), 214.

RETROSPECTIVE

30

Portraits

Judging historical greatness is a difficult and complex appraisal of the blending of public accomplishment and private virtue. And in doing so consensus is probably the least reliable guide to truth. Nonetheless, consensus cannot be overlooked; the perceptions of a man's contemporaries and the estimates of those who closely followed him yield insights that are not otherwise available. These insights are tested in acid, which the mere passage of time affords, and the result we call history.

In a backward glance at the century-and-a-half chronicle of the Missouri Supreme Court, at least four persons stand out as the giants of that bench. In addition, there must be included in any roster of the "greats" an "also-ran." This is John Brooks Henderson, and it is a scandal even in an age inclined to despise and reject its past that he has been forgotten. Nominated to the supreme court in 1862, as part of the "clean sweep" of the bench by the union-opting convention, Henderson declined judicial office and instead accepted a commission as a major general. While in the process of assembling his brigade, he was named by acting Governor Hall to succeed Missouri's Trusten Polk, who had been expelled from the United States Senate for disloyalty. In Washington, he found himself one of the youngest members of the Senate. There, after election to a full term in 1863, he wrote and introduced the Thirteenth Amendment to the Constitution, which abolished slavery finally and constitutionally. Even though his previous political career had been that of a proslavery but pro-Union Democrat, Henderson took the action because of his conviction that the amendment had the best chance of success under the sponsorship of a senator from a slave-holding state.

Even so, six votes were cast against it in the Senate, and substantial opposition in the House showed in a 119–56 vote in January 1865. By December 1865, the requisite three-quarters of the states (including eight "reconstructed" ones) had ratified, and Henderson's great work was added to the Constitution. Even so, his historic impact was not at an end. He happened to be in the Pike County Circuit Court the day Father Cummings was arraigned (see chap. 12) and persuaded the priest to change his plea to not guilty, thereby setting the stage for the constitutional confrontation in *Missouri v. Cummings.* Later and despite intense pressure he voted not guilty in the impeachment trial of Andrew Johnson and was burned in effigy from one end of Missouri to the other. He also served as counsel for Mrs. Minor in her futile effort (see chap. 14) to have women declared voters under an expansive view of the Fourteenth Amendment.

After unsuccessfully seeking the governorship in 1875, he moved to Washington where he died in 1913. Even though a Virginian, he lies far from his native and adopted states in Greenwood Cemetery in Brooklyn with John F. Kennedy's *Profiles in Courage* virtually the sole testimonial to his record.

HAMILTON GAMBLE

First and foremost on the formal roll of honor is Hamilton Rowan Gamble. He is there for two reasons: First, in the turbulent spring of 1861, it was his voice and presence in the supposedly "secession" convention that was critically important in holding Missouri in the Union. His second laurel is judicial: the dissenting opinion in the first *Dred Scott* case, which in any view of the matter was superbly right on both the law of the matter and the legitimacy of the judicial process, especially when contrasted with Judge William Scott's activist opportunism, which was frankly based on political "circumstances" and expediency.

Citing eight cases running back to the first volume of the Missouri Reports, Gamble regarded the question as settled by prior adjudications of the court: "In this State, it has been recognized, from the beginning of the government . . . that a master who takes his slave to reside in a State or Territory where slavery is prohibited, thereby emancipates his slave."[1]

The best lawyer in the court, Gamble sardonically fortified his position with citations from the slave-holding states of Louisiana, Mississippi, and Kentucky. He also added a barb noting that these decisions had been framed "when the public mind was tranquil."[2] It was a pity that his citations and his opinion did not prevail.

HENRY LAMM

If not the greatest, certainly the most quotable member of the Supreme Court of Missouri was Henry Lamm, "the Sage of Sedalia." Born in Ohio, Lamm came to Missouri after the Civil War, read law and was admitted to the bar in 1871. Elected to the court in 1904, as a result of the great "Teddy" Roosevelt sweep (after an unsuccessful try in 1902), Lamm ran for governor on the Republican ticket in 1916, losing by a mere two thousand votes. Nevertheless, he left an indelible memorial of his mind and faith in the Missouri Reports, and hardly a term of court passes without his opinions being quoted in briefs and oral argument.

Henry Lamm's prose provided him a lasting remembrance. Long after the accomplishments of what might have been the Lamm administration faded, his sparkling sequence of aphorisms embellishing the Missouri Reports constitute not only an enduring legacy but a bottomless quarry for brief writers in search of a good quote. For example, "One of the inherent powers of a court of equity is the right to act with good sense."[3]

Federal District Judge Howard Sachs has sifted the record to establish Judge Lamm's literary hegemony on his old court. In a Lexis-aided retrieval, Lamm is established as a "quotable" appellate judge surpassing James Kent, Lemuel Shaw, and standing second only to Oliver Wendell Holmes as a fortifying source.[4]

Any lawyer who has struggled with the problem of fraud will

1. Scott v. Emerson, 15 Mo. 577, 589–90 (1852).
2. *Id.* at 591.
3. State *ex rel.* Connors v. Shelton, 142 S.W. 417, 421 (Mo. en banc 1911).
4. Howard Sachs, "Lexis Brightens Memory of the Sage of Sedalia," 32 J. Mo. B. (1976): 31–37, 60.

welcome Lamm's luminous disquisition on perception and proof:
"In a pinch, in court or out, much is seen through a keyhole, or,
put otherwise, some one illuminating fact often throws a gleam
of light into the obscure corners of litigation to aid the eye of the
chancellor, precisely as a flash of lightening on a dark night re-
veals the landscape to a bewildered traveller."[5] Moreover, Lamm
applied his insight in backing up trust-busting Attorney General
Herbert Hadley:

> Now in investigating fraud it is elementary that courts tolerate a wide
> latitude and a minute search; for fraud, originating in oblique cunning,
> is often deeply laid away and may be got at alone by the keenest scru-
> tiny, but acute probing, and sometimes by the aid of indirection, a
> weighing and sifting of motives, and, again, the putting together of
> trivial circumstances may furnish persuasive evidence of fraud.[6]

Lamm as a no-nonsense judge is always well worth citing. On
the necessity of an actual case or controversy: "We do not sit as a
moot court to determine speculative questions for the benefit of
some other case in judgment at some other time. . . . We do not
sit in the comedy of Much Ado about Nothing, if we know it in
advance." Along the same lines were Judge Lamm's insights on
procedures and general principles: The rules of appellate practice
"fill no office of mere red tape, or as a show of surface routine. . . .
They have substance, and carry on their face the obvious purpose
to aid appellate courts in getting at the right of a cause." And in a
borrowed aphorism: "Presumptions . . . may be looked on as the
bats of the law, flitting in the twilight, but disappearing in the
sunshine of actual facts."[7] And, again on flexibility:

> General rules of court, like general principles of law, are subject to
> exceptions when justice cries out for the exception. Court rules are
> mere ends to the attainment of justice, and are not to be twisted into
> instruments of injustice. Courts, about the exalted office of dispensing
> justice, are not to have their functions starved or atrophied by a mere
> phrase or rule in an exceptional case.[8]

5. Howard v. Scott, 125 S.W. 1158, 1158 (Mo. Div. 1 1910).
6. State v. Standard Oil Co., 91 S.W. 1062, 1071 (Mo. en banc 1906).
7. State *ex rel.* Fischer v. Thomas, 155 S.W. 401, 402–3 (Mo. en banc 1913);
Sullivan v. Holbrook, 109 S.W. 668, 670 (Mo. Div. 1 1908); Mackowik v. Kansas
City R.R., 94 S.W. 256, 262 (Mo. Div. 1 1906).
8. Jeude v. Sims, 166 S.W. 1048, 1055 (Mo. en banc 1914).

Lamm's great aphorisms, happily excerpted, selected, and preserved between hard covers,[9] may obtain a new stature in an age which prizes permissiveness and autonomy as the high traditional freedom. Remarkable here was his prophetic condemnation of constructive contempt (see chap. 26) and his disquisition on habeas corpus, subsequently quoted in the context of a St. Louis civil rights controversy:

> Wherefore, when the great writ goes down—a writ whose origin is lost in the dawn of English history, whose final and triumphant establishment was a landmark in the evolution of civil liberty, making the hearts of its lovers leap for joy—to the prisoner, the doors of jail open; he comes into court with his shackles dropped; and the cause of his imprisonment, the very marrow of it, is laid bare to the utmost verge and minutiae permitted by written law.[10]

Lamm's talent included an ability to stimulate his colleagues to emulate him. Thus, in the "Missouri Mule Case," a Springfield intersection accident wherein the defendant's mule put a leg through the wheel of the plaintiff's buggy to $5 damages, the latter sum being awarded by a Justice of the Peace and affirmed by the Circuit Court and Court of Appeals, was reversed by the usually sedate and sobersided Judge W. W. Graves in Lammesque terms:

> This case involves the magnificent sum of five dollars. . . .
> As we gather from the facts, the plaintiff has been successful throughout from the justice's court up to the present. In the Court of Appeals his success was by a divided court. In this court he stands behind the fortification of his judgment and submits his case here without brief. A yellow slip of paper found in these here bears the ominous inscription "The Celebrated Mule Case" and nothing more. Why we were thus enlightened by the otherwise silent monitor we know not. It at least admonishes us to look well to the facts . . .
> The use of a halter with a rein of five or six feet is of such long standing that expert testimony has no place in this case. . . . The proof made in this case failed to show any negligence, and the judgment from start to finish should have been for the defendant.

9. Fred C. Mullinix, ed., *Legal Philology: Epigrams and Excerpts from the Legal Opinions of Hon. Henry Lamm.*

10. *Ex parte* Clark, 106 S.W. 990, 996 (Mo. en banc 1907).

We regret to feel constrained to abruptly terminate "The Celebrated Mule Case" but it should have been so determined long ago.[11]

LAURANCE MASTICK HYDE

Ask any aging judge or lawyer for a contemporary courtroom estimate of the great names of the Missouri Supreme Court, and in the response one name is almost invariably the first tendered: Laurance Mastick Hyde.

Born in Princeton, Missouri, the son of a congressman and brother of a member of the Herbert Hoover cabinet, Hyde came to the law by both birth and training. A product of the University of Missouri, he entered the court through a 1931 commissionership; the infirmities of the old political system were painfully demonstrated three years later when he ran as a Republican for a seat on the court, being overwhelmingly defeated by a manifestly inferior candidate who had the good fortune of being a Democrat. Nonetheless, his service and stature are also an enduring tribute to the Missouri nonpartisan court plan as the first judge appointed thereunder (1943) and rendering distinguished service, which would not have been possible save for the plan—as the 1934 election so painfully demonstrated.

Hyde was a surpassingly handsome man. His sweetness of temper and instinctive kindness were appropriately caught in the masculine beauty of his face. Memorialized in a chair at the University of Missouri School of Law, his judicial reputation ran far beyond the borders of his native state where his contributions to the administration of justice (through procedural reform and judicial selection) alone sufficed to enshrine his memory. Typical of a truly international reputation was his selection to chair the American Bar Association meetings held at the Inns of Court when the association met in London in 1957.

This laurel capped a number of tributes beyond Missouri's borders. Here a component was his unobtrusive work in the Restatement of the American Law Institute. Another more formal tribute was the retirement encomium of the American Judicature Society: "It is well known to every knowledgeable person that Judge Hyde's stature has been nationwide and worldwide, and

11. Lyman v. Dale, 117 SW 352, 354 (1914).

that the influence of his forward-looking ideas and leadership have extended to every part of our country and beyond."[12]

MATHIAS MCGIRK

Appointed in 1820 and serving for the next two decades, McGirk bore the title "president" (that of "chief justice" was not constitutionalized until 1875) with great dignity.

He is something of a man of mystery. No likeness whatsoever of him is extant, and such vital statistics as we have come from a replacement gravestone. Born in Virginia in 1790, he came to Missouri at an unknown date. In 1813, he was appointed to the Territorial Council, something of an upper house of the territorial legislature. In 1818, while serving in that capacity, he successfully sponsored the "reception" statute whereby the common law of England became the law of the Missouri Territory and displaced the French law which previously ruled civil disputes in that area.

Upon Missouri's admission to the union, Governor McNair appointed him to the new state supreme court and signed his commission November 14, 1820. The date was critically important since the rules of that tribunal subsequently provided that "the oldest judge in point of service shall be the President of the Supreme Court." Though younger in age to his colleagues on that early three-man bench, precedence came from his commission (Judge Cook's was signed two days later and that of Judge John Jones almost a fortnight subsequently).

His first colleagues left the bench shortly after appointment by death or resignation; however, McGirk remained at his post for two decades providing an element of continuity and stability which insured the distinctive regional cachet of Missouri law. His correspondence and bench notes have been lost, and his will perished when the Montgomery County courthouse burned toward the end of the nineteenth century.

However, McGirk did leave an imperishable memento of his public service in the Missouri Reports. In one opinion, *State v. Fry et al.*,[13] grappled with the problem that had beset Chief Jus-

---

12. Henry Andrae, "Laurance Mastick Hyde."
13. 4 Mo. 120 (1835).

tice Marshall in the *Dartmouth College* case—the consistency of divorce with the contract clause of the federal constitution—and resolved it better. As McGirk demonstrated, legislatively granted divorce, whatever the English precedent, was analytically repugnant not only to the federal contracts clause but also to the doctrine of separation of powers. It was a special tribute to his opinion that the Missouri Constitution was subsequently amended to bar the General Assembly from granting divorces and transferring that function to the civil courts.[14]

14. Mo. Const. of 1820, amend. IX.

31

Miniatures

Professor Arthur Schlesinger, Sr., has told us that the spirit of an age may be better embodied in its secondary figures than the men who stand in the front rank. In this context the rich tapestry which constitutes the history of the Missouri Supreme Court may more easily be glimpsed in those members of the court whose lives capture the spirit of the time in which they lived and thereby provide an especial thread in the court's tapestry—in spite of never having had a *Dred Scott* case thrust upon them.

ABIEL LEONARD

In his classic *American Dilemma*, Gunnar Myrdal singled out the duello as the quintessential barbarism of early American society and, after its fashion, something of the Siamese twin of the lynch law. Representative of this spirit was Judge Abiel Leonard who joined the court in 1855. In his way he embodied the raw spirit of Jacksonian frontier democracy when he entered the court as one of the first elected (rather than appointed) judges; more than that he had actually killed a man in a duel.

So had President Andrew Jackson and Senator Thomas Hart Benton. So had many other prominent public personages. Indeed, Missouri had long struggled with the problem, for in the ethos of the time fighting a duel frequently involved far less social disgrace than the failure to fight one. The initial territorial prohibition against dueling was easily circumvented by going outstate to fight one, hence "Bloody Island" on the Illinois side of the Mississippi became a favorite battleground for Missouri duelists. Dueling itself had been forbidden since the territorial days, but legislative frustration with evasive tactics was evident in the prologue to a new and comprehensive ban passed in 1822:

> Whereas, experience has evinced the existing remedy for the suppression of the barbarous custom of duelling is inadequate to the purpose, and the progress and consequences of the evil has been so destructive as to require an effort on the part of the general assembly to arrest the vice, the result of ignorance and barbarity, justified neither by the precepts of morality nor by the dictates of reason.[1]

Hence, the new law punished the mere sending of a challenge and penalized inflicting death in a duel as murder with minimum punishment entailing loss of civil rights.

But Leonard was also atypical. He came from New England rather than the upper South, which was the matrix of most migrants to the state. More than that, he was mousy and unimpressive in a culture that prized leonine flamboyance (exemplified in Jackson and Benton) in public personages. A five-foot one-hundred-pound Yankee, he was remembered as a "small man physically, so ugly as to attract attention, but with a lion's voice that challenged contradiction."[2]

Major Taylor Berry, postmaster at Fayette, made the error of misreading the unimpressive exterior. As circuit attorney in Fayette, Leonard presented the case against Berry when the latter was indicted for forgery and perjury. After acquittal, Berry took a whip and gave Leonard a "raw-hiding" outside the courthouse.[3] Events then moved with the inexorability of a Greek tragedy, Leonard dispatching the traditional challenge. "Sir: I demand a personal interview with you. My friend, Mr. Boggs will make the necessary arrangements on my part. Yours etc. A. Leonard."[4]

1. Act of December 13, 1822, Mo. Laws 1825–1827.

2. Judge John F. Phillips, "Reminiscences of Some Deceased Lawyers of Central Missouri," *Journal of the Missouri Bar* 32 (1976): 280–81.

3. William Colmer, "Abiel Leonard," *Missouri Historical Review* 27 (1933): 217–24.

4. Abiel Leonard to Taylor Berry, June 26, 1824, quoted from William V. Bay, *Reminiscences of the Bench and Bar of Missouri*, 361.

Berry accepted but noted that his action had originated "in passion"[5] and took the precaution of placing Leonard under a $5,000 peace bond. Bond notwithstanding, the duelists repaired to "some point, either in Kentucky, Tennessee, or Arkansas . . . most convenient to the town of New Madrid."[6] Then on September 1, 1824, they met at ten paces with pistols drawn, and at the first exchange of fire Berry fell, mortally wounded. Upon his return to Fayette, Leonard was tried for violation of one dueling prohibition, fined $150 and perpetually barred from voting and from any office of trust or honor in the service of the state.

Nonetheless, the circumstances of the duel combined with Leonard's rising popularity caused a flurry of petitions to descend on the General Assembly. Before the year was out, Governor Bates reluctantly signed a special resolution that restored Leonard's civil rights and permitted Leonard to be elected—thirty years later—to the state supreme court in 1855.[7] He served for two years, turning out some opinions of remarkable scholarship. He had other distinctions. It was his counsel in the secession crisis of 1861, which provided critical assistance to Hamilton Gamble, persuading the latter to seize power and hold the state in the Union. He was also the first supreme court judge to acquire an academic patina, being elected "Professor of Pleading, Practice, Evidence and Criminal Jurisprudence" at Washington University in April of 1860. Leonard declined the appointment. Typically, he seldom mentioned the Berry duel, except to say that he never regretted it.

SHEPARD BARCLAY

Shepard Barclay was in a sense involved in Missouri legal history while still a child. Two years after his birth, his mother and father were divorced by an 1849 legislative act—one of the last such dissolutions granted. Upon attaining his majority in 1868, Barclay (born Shepard Hill) changed his surname to that of his mother's second husband.[8]

He entered St. Louis University at the age of fifteen in 1862,

5. *Id.*
6. *Id.*
7. Mo. Laws, *Private Acts* (1824), chapter 13.
8. See generally Lawrence G. Crahan, "An Intimate View of Judge Shepard Barclay," *Missouri Supreme Court Historical Journal* 1, (Summer 1988): 5–9.

graduating at the head of his class in 1866. After graduation he studied law at the University of Virginia, graduating in 1869 along with two southerners, William Champe Marshall of Mississippi and James Britton Gantt of Georgia, both of whom subsequently served with him on the Missouri Supreme Court.

The service of the trio was a striking example of the state's lingering southern acculturation, and Barclay's upper-class credentials were amply attested by his grand tour, which followed his second graduation. It not only afforded an encounter with European culture and a view of the downfall of Louis Napoleon, but it also provided a writing apprenticeship in the form of dispatches to the St. Louis papers on the Franco-Prussian War.

Returning home in 1872, Barclay formed a law partnership with his Virginia classmate, William Champe Marshall. He was elected to the St. Louis Circuit Court in 1884, and three years later a testimonial from his colleagues there: "An intimate knowledge of your merits, [makes] you particularly qualified for the Supreme Court [of Missouri]."[9]

Barclay threw his hat in the ring, and after what the *St. Louis Republic* called "one of the most hotly contested fights ever known in the political history of Missouri"[10] won the Democratic nomination for the supreme court seat at the Democratic state convention. He swept to victory in the 1892 election leading a Democratic ticket that included the formidable David R. Francis as the gubernatorial nominee.

Barclay, with his good-humored face and mutton-chop sideburns looked like a typical successful establishmentarian. The man beneath the mask was far more complex. He converted to Catholicism while a student at St. Louis University but gradually unconverted, attending a protest meeting to the Vatican I pronouncement of papal infallibility while on his European tour. Married in 1873, the first ceremony was a clandestine Catholic one and the second a glittering society event the next day at the Episcopal cathedral. The marriage had lyric and lasting quality, but Mrs. Barclay, aside from an occasional visit to Jefferson City,

9. Clarence Miller, *Shepard Barclay*, 48.
10. *Id.*, 51.

remained in St. Louis, permitting the supreme court judge to rusticate in solitude.

He resigned from the court in January 1898 "in order to attempt to earn something for my support when I reached old age."[11] He returned to the practice of law, forming McKeign, Barclay, and Watts—a highly respected firm—but did not practice law long. Governor Dockery appointed him to the St. Louis Court of Appeals in 1901. He served there until 1903, leaving to form Barclay, Fauntelroy, and Collier, a firm which entered a formidable defense to the sanctions proposed upon his in-laws' chemical complex under the state antitrust law.[12]

Barclay was the first man to serve on all three judicial levels, but the indecisive oscillation between bench and bar continued. In 1922 he ran for circuit judge on the Democratic ticket but was defeated in what had become the chronically Republican city of St. Louis. His variegated judicial career had another analog in Barclay's complex makeup. Doubtless the sting of defeat for the bench in 1922 was assuaged three years later by a very special consolation when he received his athletic letter—sixty years after his service as the star pitcher of the St. Louis University team of 1866–1867. The *Post-Dispatch* paid an editorial tribute:

Judge Barclay—Letterman
We'll bet, not having heard the Judge at length on the subject, that one of his favorite stories is how he pitched old St. Louis U. to victory just after the civil war. We'll bet his most prized trophy is the white S. L. just now awarded him. Honorary L.L.D.'s are puny awards compared to it.[13]

A few months later in the last interview granted before his death, both he and Monsignor Martin Brennan, a local pastor, reminisced how they had dueled in a 54–33 encounter between students from St. Louis University and Christian Brothers College (now a high school but then a collegiate institution) in the days when pitchers threw underhand and fielders had no gloves.

11. *Id.*, 56.
12. State *ex rel.* Jones v. Mallinkrodt Chemical Works, 156 S.W. 967 (Mo. en banc 1913) aff'd, 238 U.S. 41 (1915). Interestingly, Barclay held the original Missouri Anti-Trust Act unconstitutional when it came before him. State *ex rel.* Attorney General v. Simmons Hardware Co., 18 S.W. 1125 (Mo. Div. 1 1892).
13. "Judge Barclay—Letterman," *St. Louis Post-Dispatch*, July 3, 1925.

"Shepard Barclay had an unusual delivery," recalled the Monsignor, "a deceptive underhanded curve ball that we could not solve."[14] Barclay died shortly after the interview and was buried from Christ Church Cathedral where he had been married. His probate inventory explained his judicial oscillation, for it listed liabilities in excess of assets of $135,000—explanation enough of a taste for good living and frequent employment changes on and off the bench.

THE PROFESSORS

The first member of the state supreme court to move from the bench to academia was Philemon Bliss, who accepted an appointment at the University of Missouri when his term expired in 1872, and who was designated dean shortly thereafter.

He was a New Englander who came to Missouri from New York and Ohio, having served as both judge and member of Congress in Ohio. President Lincoln had appointed him chief judge of the Dakota Territory during the Civil War, and with the peace he settled in Buchanan County as probate judge.

This was the time when Dean Christopher Columbus Langdell was revolutionizing American legal education from the Harvard Law School, but Dean Bliss ensured that legal education would take the same path in Columbia that had guided his court in Jefferson City—stability, continuity, and predictability. There were changes, however. It was under Bliss that the organic beginnings of an autonomous law school took place with the formation of the Department of Law in 1872. Bliss served as dean for seventeen years and wrote "an elaborate treatise upon pleading which has become a standard work on the subject."[15]

The judicial-academic tradition continued with Bliss's successor, Alexander Martin of St. Louis, who had been one of the first commissioners of the state supreme court and a Harvard Law School graduate in 1858. Succeeding Bliss in 1889 he stayed at the helm for thirteen years, guiding the law school until 1902.

The reinforced judicial component of the law school was marked by a significant index of later times. Folklore has it that the custom of rising as the professor took the podium began with Dean

14. *St. Louis Globe Democrat*, November 24, 1927.
15. William V. Bay, *Bench and Bar*, 379.

Bliss, who was still obviously accustomed to the tradition of all present in the court rising as the judge ascended the bench. The custom was reinforced with Martin's ascension as Bliss's successor and lasted until the turbulence of the mid–1960s when, as a result of students' discontent, it was no longer observed.

THE WOUNDED CONFEDERATE

A native Georgian, Judge James Britton Gantt enlisted in the Confederate Army at sixteen. He was wounded in three battles: Gettysburg (twice), Cedar Creek (site of Sheridan's famous ride), and the Wilderness. After being discharged for medical reasons, he attended the University of Virginia Law School along with William Marshall of Mississippi and Shepard Barclay of Missouri; all graduated in 1869 and ultimately practiced law in Missouri. All three sat on the state supreme court.

Gantt was the only Democrat to attempt to run for the governorship from that bench, entering the lists in the 1904 contest. He picked a poor year, for the ambitious St. Louis prosecutor, Joseph Folk, was already in the field, and the St. Louis "boodle" scandals put the Democrats in poor repute. Gantt baited Folk mercilessly from the bench when the latter argued the "boodler" appeals. The corruption issue caused Gantt to fall between two stools with both the organization stalwarts and the reformers seeing him as an enemy. A similar hostility came from both sides in a decision on church government, which perhaps entailed not only the loss of the governorship but also political defeat when he ran for a third term on the court in 1910.[16]

DUE PROCESS, FREE PRESS

Archelaus Woodson, nephew of the "Redemption" Governor, Silas Woodson, had the good fortune of writing one of the great libertarian opinions of his court in the course of an otherwise undistinguished career.

The occasion was *Ex Parte Nelson*, a case involving the maverick Judge Joseph Guthrie of the Jackson County Circuit Court, the divorcing Clevengers, a couple who quickly disappeared into obscurity, and the owner of the *Kansas City Star*, William Rock-

16. North Todd Gentry, "Some Missouri Judges I Have Known," 342–57.

hill Nelson.[17] The controversy opened when an article in the *Star* stated that Judge Guthrie had to refuse to dismiss the divorce proceeding until counsel fees had been paid. Nelson, as publisher, was promptly cited for contempt and ordered to show cause why he should not be punished. He appeared and pleaded, virtually admitting the facts charged in the citation. Judge Guthrie then opened the drawer of his bench and took out a manuscript—prepared the night before—and read an opinion finding Nelson guilty and sentencing him to a day in jail.

The issue of whether constructive contempt was compatible with evolving constitutional values and the related legitimacy of a procedure that reversed the traditional sequence of proof and punishment provided an issue far transcending the facts of the case. "Nelson Contempt Case Argued in Supreme Court"[18] ran a prominently headlined story in the *St. Louis Post-Dispatch*. The story reported an exchange during argument when O. H. Dean, representing Judge Guthrie, asserted that the bar had cheered the Guthrie ruling. Judge John Broom shot back, "And the mob cheered Pilate when he sentenced Christ to crucifixion."[19]

Broom's response was a good index of things to come. On June 2, 1913, the court ordered Nelson released from punishment. The court found that Nelson had been guilty of contempt, but his sentence had been vitiated by the pretrial conclusion that dispensed with a proof before judgment. Woodson's authorities ranged from the common law, the Constitution, and the Book of Revelations. After noting the lofty spiritual source, Woodson continued:

> Returning to earth: the authorities are uniform in holding that those constitutional provisions are applicable to every form of procedure where the life, liberty, or property of a person is sought to be taken from him. . . .
> . . . even the most guilty are entitled to a fair and impartial trial before they can be legally pronounced guilty. [The defendant] may have proclaimed his guilt from the housetops [but] nevertheless, he must be accorded the same fair and impartial trial, according to the forms of law that would be accorded a king, a prince or a potentate.[20]

17. 157 S.W. 794 (Mo. en banc 1913).
18. "Nelson Contempt Case Argued," *St. Louis Post-Dispatch*, May 4, 1913.
19. *Id.*
20. *Nelson*, 575 S.W. at 808.

Appendix: Judges and Commissioners

JUDGES OF THE MISSOURI SUPREME COURT

The judges of the Missouri Supreme Court are listed below in the order of their service, according to the *Official Manual of the State of Missouri*. The judge with the longest tenure is Caleb Abnew Leedy, Jr., thirty-two years, and the shortest belongs to Clarence Alexander Burney, six weeks.

1. Matthias McGirk	1820–1841
2. John Dillard Cook	1820–1823
3. John Rice Jones	1820–1824
4. Rufus Pettibone	1823–1845
5. George Tompkins	1824–1845
6. Robert Wash	1825–1837
7. William Barclay Napton	1839–1851, 1857–1861, and 1873–1880
8. William Scott	1841–1862
9. Priestly Haggin McBride	1845–1849
10. John Ferguson Ryland	1849–1857
11. James Harvey Birch	1849–1851
12. Hamilton Rowan Gamble	1851–1855
13. Abiel Leonard	1855–1857
14. John Crowley Richardson	1857–1859
15. Ephraim Brevard Ewing	1859–1861 and 1872–1873

209

16.	Barton Bates	1862–1865
17.	William Van Ness Bay	1862–1865
18.	John Debos Sharp Dryden	1862–1865
19.	David Wagner	1865–1876
20.	Walter L. Lovelace	1865–1866
21.	Nathaniel Holmes	1865–1868
22.	Thomas James Clark Fagg	1866–1869
23.	James Baker	1868–1869
24.	Philemon Bliss	1868–1872
25.	Warren Currier	1868–1871
26.	Washington Adams	1871–1874
27.	Henry M. Vories	1872–1876
28.	Thomas Adiel Sherwood	1872–1902
29.	Edward Augustus Lewis	1874
30.	Warwick Hough	1874–1884
31.	Elijah Hise Norton	1876–1888
32.	John Ward Henry	1876–1886
33.	Robert D. Ray	1880–1890
34.	Francis Marion Black	1884–1894
35.	Theodore Brace	1886–1900
36.	Shepard Barclay	1888–1898
37.	James Britton Gantt	1890–1910
38.	John Lilburn Thomas	1890–1893
39.	George Bonnett MacFarlane	1890–1898
40.	Gavon Drummond Burgess	1892–1910
41.	Waltour Moore Robinson	1894–1904
42.	William Muir Williams	1898–1899
43.	William Champe Marshall	1898–1906
44.	Leroy B. Valliant	1898–1912
45.	James David Fox	1902–1910
46.	Henry Lamm	1904–1914
47.	Waller Washington Graves	1906–1928
48.	Archelaus Marius Woodson	1906–1926
49.	John Chilton Brown	1910–1915
50.	John Kennish	1910–1912
51.	Franklin Ferris	1910–1912
52.	Henry Whitelaw Bond	1912–1919
53.	Charles Breckenridge Faris	1912–1919
54.	Robert Franklin Walker	1912–1930
55.	James Thomas Blair	1914–1924
56.	Charles G. Revelle	1915–1917
57.	Fred Lincoln Williams	1916–1920

58.	Richard Livingston Goode	1919–1920
59.	John Isaac Williamson	1919–1920
60.	Conway Elder	1920–1922
61.	David Elmore Blair	1920–1922
62.	Edward Higbee	1920–1922
63.	William Talliaferro Ragland	1922–1932
64.	John Turner White	1922–1932
65.	Frank Ely Atwood	1925–1935
66.	Robert William Otto	1925–1926
67.	Ernest S. Gantt	1926–1946
68.	North Todd Gentry	1928
69.	William Francis Frank	1928–1938
70.	Berryman Henwood	1930–1932
71.	George Robb Ellison	1930–1957
72.	Charles Thomas Hays	1932–1942
73.	Earnest Moss Tipton	1932–1955
74.	Clarence Alexander Burney	1932–1933
75.	Caleb Abner Leedy, Jr.	1933–1964
76.	Walter D. Coles	1935
77.	John Caskie Collet	1935–1937
78.	James Marsh Douglas	1937–1950
79.	Albert M. Clark	1938–1950
80.	Ray B. Lucas	1938
81.	Laurance Mastick Hyde	1942–1966
82.	Roscoe P. Conkling	1947–1954
83.	Sidna Poage Dalton	1950–1965
84.	Frank Hollingsworth	1950–1964
85.	Henry J. Westhues	1954–1963
86.	Henry I. Eager	1955–1969
87.	Clem F. Storckman	1955–1970
88.	Lawrence Holman	1963–1977
89.	Fred L. Henley	1964–1978
90.	James A. Finch, Jr.	1964–1979
91.	Robert True Donnelly	1965–1988
92.	Robert Eldridge Seiler	1966–1982
93.	June P. Morgan	1969–1982
94.	John E. Bardgett	1970–1982
95.	Albert L. Rendlen	1977–1992
96.	Joseph J. Simeone	1978–1979
97.	Warren Dee Welliver	1979–1989
98.	Andrew Jackson Higgins	1979–1991
99.	George F. Gunn, Jr.	1982–1985

100. William Howard Billings	1982–1991
101. Charles Blakey Blackmar	1982–1992
102. Edward D. Robertson, Jr.	1985–
103. Ann Kettering Covington	1988–
104. John C. Holstein	1989–
105. Duane Benton	1991–
106. Elwood Thomas	1991–
107. William Ray Price, Jr.	1992–
108. Stephen N. Limbaugh, Jr.	1992–

THE COMMISSIONERS

The commissioners of the Missouri Supreme Court may well be seen as the most distinctive factor in the history of that tribunal. The commissioner system gave the court the means of keeping its docket current thanks to a group of hardworking men who regularly wrote more than their share of opinions. Moreover, cases with long transcripts, swollen records, and difficult points of decision were routinely assigned to them. Their number included men with distinguished preappointment careers, and many went on after commissioner service to noteworthy achievement. A point of pride has been the freedom from scandal, misfeasance, or similar ignominious misbehavior by any commissioner. More than that, the commissioners kept aloof from any of the personality conflicts that from time to time inevitably racked the court such as the Gantt feud (see chap. 23). Perhaps institutional constraints helped. "All a lowly commissioner could do in the midst of that bitter struggle," recalled Judge Paul Barrett, "was to keep out of sight."

The list of commissioners follows. Included are both groups: those appointed under the first authorization of 1883–1884 and those appointed under the second, 1911–1980:

1. Charles A. Winslow	1882–1883
2. John F. Philips	1882–1885
3. Alexander Martin	1882–1886
4. H. Clay Ewing	1883–1886
5. David D. DeArmond	1885–1886
6. Henry W. Bond	1911–1912
7. James T. Blair	1911–1914
8. Reuben F. Roy	1911–1919
9. Stephens S. Brown	1911–1923
10. Fred L. Williams	1913–1916
11. Robert T. Railey	1915–1927

12.	John Turner White	1917–1922
13.	Norman A. Mozley	1919–1921
14.	William T. Ragland	1919–1922
15.	Charles Edwin Small	1919–1924
16.	Albert L. Reeves	1921–1923
17.	Walter Naylor Davis	1923
18.	Edward Higbee	1923–1929
19.	James D. Lindsay	1923–1930
20.	Alfred Morton Seddon	1924–1931
21.	Berryman Henwood	1927–1930
22.	George Robb Ellison	1927–1931
23.	Walter Naylor Davis	1927–1931
24.	James A. Cooley	1929–1941
25.	Charles L. Ferguson	1930–1939
26.	Henry J. Westhues	1939–1954
27.	John T. Fitzsimmons	1931–1934
28.	John Thomas Sturgis	1931–1935
29.	Laurance Mastick Hyde	1931–1943
30.	Walter H. Bohling	1934–1963
31.	John H. Bradley	1935–1950
32.	Sidna Poage Dalton	1939–1950
33.	Paul W. Barrett	1941–1972
34.	Paul Van Osdol	1943–1959
35.	Frank P. Aschemeyer	1950–1951
36.	Lue C. Lozier	1950–1955
37.	Cullen Coil	1951–1964
38.	Alden A. Stockard	1954–1982
39.	Lawrence Holman	1955–1963
40.	Norwin D. Houser	1959–1978
41.	Jack Pence Pritchard	1963–1972
42.	Robert Rucker Welborn	1963–1981
43.	Andrew Jackson Higgins	1964–1979

Bibliography

Andrae, Henry. "Laurance Mastick Hyde." *Missouri Supreme Court Historical Bulletin* 2 (Summer 1982): 2–5.

Annals of the Congress of the United States, 1851. Vol. 37. Washington, D.C.: Gales & Seaton, 1820–1821.

Arnold, Morris. *Unequal Laws unto a Savage Race.* Fayetteville: University of Arkansas Press, 1988.

Barclay, Thomas B. "The Liberal Republican Movement in Missouri." *Missouri Historical Review* 20 (October 1925): 3–44, 45–78, 262–94.

Bay, William V. *Reminiscences of the Bench and Bar of Missouri.* St. Louis: F. H. Thomas & Co., 1870.

Bellamy, Donnie D. "Free Blacks in Antebellum Missouri, 1820–1860." *Missouri Historical Review* 67 (1973): 198–226.

The Bench and Bar of St. Louis, Kansas City, Jefferson City and Other Missouri Cities; Biographical Sketches. St. Louis: American Biographical Publishing Co., 1884.

Bradley, Harold Charles. "In Defense of John Cummings." *Missouri Historical Review* 57 (October 1962): 1–15.

Brockhoff, Dorothy. "James M. Douglas." *Washington University Magazine* 38 (Fall 1967): 43–47.

Bryan, John A. "The Blow Family and Their Slave Dred Scott." *Missouri Historical Society Bulletin* 4 (1948): 223–31.

Chaney, Walter L. "The True Story of 'Old Drum.'" *Missouri Historical Review* 19 (1925): 313–24.

Clark, Albert M. "The Supreme Court of Missouri." *Missouri Historical Review* 37 (1943): 162–68.

Crahan, Lawrence J. "An Intimate View of Judge Shepard Barclay." *Missouri Supreme Court Historical Bulletin* 2 (Summer 1990): 5–9.

Culmer, Frederic A. "The Leonard-Berry Duel of 1824." *Missouri Historical Review* 49 (1955): 357–59.

Dargo, George. *Jefferson's Louisiana: Politics and the Clash of Legal Traditions.* Cambridge: Harvard University Press, 1975.

Fagg, Thomas J. C. "The Pike County Circuit Court." *Missouri Historical Review* 1 (1907): 191–97.

Faherty S. J., William. "American Hero Anonymous: John Cummings and the Iron-Clad Oath (1840–1873)." *The St. Louis Bar Journal* 27 (Spring 1981): 56–58.

Fehrenbacher, Don E. *The Dred Scott Case.* New York: Oxford University Press, 1978.

Foley, William E. "Slave Freedom Suits before Dred Scott: The Case of Marie Jean Scypion's Descendants." *Missouri Historical Review* 79 (1984): 1–23.

Gentry, North Todd. "Some Missouri Judges I Have Known." *Missouri Historical Review* 34 (1940): 342–57.

Hamilton, W. J. "The Relief Movement in Missouri, 1820–1822." *Missouri Historical Review* 22 (1927): 51–92.

Hill, Craig. "The Honey War." *Pioneer America* 14 (1922): 81–88.

Hyde, Laurance. "Historical Review of the Judicial System of Missouri." In *Vernon's Annotated Missouri Statutes.* Kansas City: Vernon Law Book, 1952.

Jackson, William Rufus. *Missouri Democracy: A History of the Party and Its Representative Members, Past and Present.* 3 vols. Chicago: S. J. Clarke Publishing Co., 1935.

James, Kent. *Commentaries on American Law.* 15th ed. New York, 1844.

King, Roy T. "Robert William Wells, Jurist, Public Servant, and Designer of the Missouri State Seal." *Missouri Historical Review* 30 (1936): 107–31.

Kirschten, Ernest. *Catfish and Crystal.* Garden City: Doubleday, 1960.

Krauthoff, L. C. "The Supreme Court of Missouri." *The Green Bag* 3 (1891): 157–90.

Laughlin, Sceva B. "Missouri Politics during the Civil War." *Missouri Historical Review* 24 (1930): 261–84.

Locke, Keltner. "A Peck of Trouble." *The St. Louis Bar Journal* 27 (Summer 1980): 50–53.

Loeb, Isidor. "Constitutions and Constitutional Conventions in Missouri." *Missouri Historical Review* 16 (1922): 189–246.

Merkel, Benjamin C. "The Slavery Issue and the Political Decline of Thomas Hart Benton, 1846–1856," *Missouri Historical Review* 38 (1944): 388–407.

Miller, Clarence E. *Shepard Barclay.* St. Louis: Privately printed, 1931.

Mullinix, Fred C., ed. *Legal Philology: Epigrams and Excerpts from the Legal Opinions of Hon. Harry Lamm, White Justice of the Supreme Court of Missouri.* St. Louis: F. H. Thomas Law Book Co., 1923.

Myrdal, Gunnar. *An American Dilemma: The Negro Problem and Modern Democracy.* New York: Harper & Bros., 1944.

Peltason, Jack. "The Missouri Plan for the Selection of Judges." *The University of Missouri Studies* 20 (1945): 3–114.

Pepper, Claude. *Pepper: Eyewitness to a Century.* San Diego: Harcourt Brace Jovanovich, 1987.

Philips, John F. "The Lawyer in Missouri: One Hundred Years Ago." *Missouri Historical Review* 13 (1919): 377–87.

Primm, James Neal. *Economic Policy in the Development of a Western State, Missouri, 1820–1860.* Cambridge: Harvard University Press, 1954.

Richardson, James D., comp. *A Compilation of the Messages and Papers of the Presidents.* 20 vols. New York: Bureau of National Literature, 1897.

Shoemaker, Floyd C. "Some Colorful Lawyers in the History of Missouri, 1804–1904." *Missouri Historical Review* 53 (1939): 125–31.

———. *Missouri's Struggle for Statehood, 1804–1821.* New York: Russell & Russell, 1943.

Soapes, Thomas F. "The Governorship 'Steal' and the Republican Revival." *Missouri Historical Society Bulletin* 32 (April 1976): 158–72.

Staley, Laura. "Suffrage Movement in St. Louis during the 1870s." *Gateway Heritage* 3 (Spring 1983): 34–41.

Stansbury, Arthur J. *Report of the Trial of James H. Peck.* Boston: Hilliard, Gray and Co., 1833.

State of Missouri. *Official Manual, State of Missouri.* Jefferson City, 1891–1987.

————. *Reports of Cases Decided by the Supreme Court of Missouri.* Jefferson City, 1821–1966.

Stevens, Walter B. *Centennial History of Missouri.* St. Louis: S. J. Clarke Publishing Co., 1921.

Thorpe, Francis, comp. and ed. *The Federal and State Constitutions, Colonial Charters, and Other Organic Laws of the States, Territories, and Colonies Now or Heretofore Forming the United States of America.* Washington: GPO, 1909.

Torrey, Jay L. *"The Supreme Court": The Trial System in Missouri.* St. Louis: Jones Publishing Co., 1892.

Watson, Richard A., and Rondal Downing. *The Politics of the Bench and Bar: Judicial Selection under the Missouri Nonpartisan Court Plan.* New York: John Wiley and Sons, 1969.

Wright, Bonnie, Robert Durant Smith, and Haden D. Smith. "And It Was Red: Missouri's New Supreme Court Building, 1907." *Missouri Historical Review* 78 (1984): 414–27.

Index